COMPUTERS AND SOCIETY

Other Books in the Current Controversies Series:

The Abortion Controversy
Alcoholism
The Disabled
Drug Trafficking
Energy Alternatives
Ethics
Europe
Family Violence
Free Speech
Gambling
Garbage and Waste
Gay Rights
Genetics and Intelligence
Gun Control
Hate Crimes
Hunger
Illegal Immigration
The Information Highway
Interventionism
Iraq
Marriage and Divorce
Nationalism and Ethnic Conflict
Police Brutality
Politicians and Ethics
Pollution
Reproductive Technologies
Sexual Harassment
Smoking
Teen Addiction
Urban Terrorism
Violence Against Women
Violence in the Media
Women in the Military
Youth Violence

COMPUTERS AND SOCIETY

David Bender, *Publisher*
Bruno Leone, *Executive Editor*

Scott Barbour, *Managing Editor*
Brenda Stalcup, *Senior Editor*

Paul A. Winters, *Book Editor*

Cover photo: © Bob Daemmrich / Uniphoto

Library of Congress Cataloging-in-Publication Data

Computers and society / Paul A. Winters, book editor.
p. cm. — (Current controversies)
Includes bibliographical references and index.
ISBN 1-56510-564-8 (alk. paper). — ISBN 1-56510-563-X (Pbk.: alk. paper)
1. Computers—Social aspects. I. Winters, Paul A., 1965– . II. Series.
QA76.9.C66C653 1997
303.48'34—dc21 97-4942
CIP

Contents

Chapter 2: How Will Computer Technology Affect the Right to Privacy?

Foreword

By definition, controversies are "discussions of questions in which opposing opinions clash" (Webster's Twentieth Century Dictionary Unabridged). Few would deny that controversies are a pervasive part of the human condition and exist on virtually every level of human enterprise. Controversies transpire between individuals and among groups, within nations and between nations. Controversies supply the grist necessary for progress by providing challenges and challengers to the status quo. They also create atmospheres where strife and warfare can flourish. A world without controversies would be a peaceful world; but it also would be, by and large, static and prosaic.

The Series' Purpose

The purpose of the Current Controversies series is to explore many of the social, political, and economic controversies dominating the national and international scenes today. Titles selected for inclusion in the series are highly focused and specific. For example, from the larger category of criminal justice, Current Controversies deals with specific topics such as police brutality, gun control, white collar crime, and others. The debates in Current Controversies also are presented in a useful, timeless fashion. Articles and book excerpts included in each title are selected if they contribute valuable, long-range ideas to the overall debate. And wherever possible, current information is enhanced with historical documents and other relevant materials. Thus, while individual titles are current in focus, every effort is made to ensure that they will not become quickly outdated. Books in the Current Controversies series will remain important resources for librarians, teachers, and students for many years.

In addition to keeping the titles focused and specific, great care is taken in the editorial format of each book in the series. Book introductions and chapter prefaces are offered to provide background material for readers. Chapters are organized around several key questions that are answered with diverse opinions representing all points on the political spectrum. Materials in each chapter include opinions in which authors clearly disagree as well as alternative opinions in which authors may agree on a broader issue but disagree on the possible solutions. In this way, the content of each volume in Current Controversies mirrors the mosaic of opinions encountered in society. Readers will quickly realize that there are many viable answers to these complex issues. By questioning each author's conclusions, students and casual readers can begin to develop the critical thinking skills so important to evaluating opinionated material.

Current Controversies is also ideal for controlled research. Each anthology in the series is composed of primary sources taken from a wide gamut of informational categories including periodicals, newspapers, books, United States and foreign government documents, and the publications of private and public organizations. Readers will find factual support for reports, debates, and research papers covering all areas of important issues. In addition, an annotated table of contents, an index, a book and periodical bibliography, and a list of organizations to contact are included in each book to expedite further research.

Perhaps more than ever before in history, people are confronted with diverse and contradictory information. During the Persian Gulf War, for example, the public was not only treated to minute-to-minute coverage of the war, it was also inundated with critiques of the coverage and countless analyses of the factors motivating U.S. involvement. Being able to sort through the plethora of opinions accompanying today's major issues, and to draw one's own conclusions, can be a complicated and frustrating struggle. It is the editors' hope that Current Controversies will help readers with this struggle.

"One area in which the optimism of computer enthusiasts comes into immediate conflict with the skepticism of critics is education."

Introduction

The first modern digital computers were developed in the 1940s for military purposes that arose during World War II. These computers filled entire rooms, and at rates of a few thousand calculations per second, they took hours to perform complex mathematical operations. In the 1970s, the first personal computers were sold. Fitting on a desktop, they were exponentially faster and more powerful than the computers that had once filled large rooms. They were also affordable to individual consumers, making it possible for many people to use them for personal, business, and academic needs. By the mid-1990s, laptop computers capable of millions of calculations per second had been developed. Currently, nearly half of American homes have a personal computer, and businesses have come to rely on computers for nearly every function. Futurists prognosticate that computers will continue to become smaller and more powerful and that they will be used in almost every facet of people's lives.

Among those who are excited and optimistic about the changes that computers will bring in the near future is Bill Gates, the founder of Microsoft, which produces much of the software that runs business and personal computers. According to Gates, now that computers are small, powerful, cheap, and affect every part of our lives, the next step will be the formation of a network connecting all of these computers to each other. On this network, which some people are calling the information highway, "computers will join together to communicate with us and for us," Gates predicts. The changes to society will be as revolutionary as those of the Industrial Age and the Renaissance, he believes. Not only will people shop and conduct business through their computers, he says, but they will also engage in every type of human activity, from reading to simply hanging out with friends. In Gates's vision, the increased level of communication made possible by computer networks will bring many benefits in the areas of business, education, and social interaction, producing widespread sharing of knowledge and wealth and a worldwide cultural renewal.

A few social critics, however, are skeptical of the futuristic optimism of computer enthusiasts such as Gates. They question whether the apparent benefits of computer technology will outweigh the potential harms. According to Christopher Scheer, a freelance writer and editor, "Technology has done nothing to lessen . . . our all-too-immediate social problems," such as environmental degradation, economic inequality, and the decline of cities. In many ways, the development of technology has exacerbated rather than ameliorated these problems, he contends, and in much the same way, the changes to society that computers will bring may be as harmful as beneficial. For instance, Scheer asserts, the communication that takes place over computer networks pales in comparison to real human interaction. Since computers tend to decrease actual human contact, he argues, their use may weaken people's sense of community and widen existing social divisions. Though it is inevitable that computers will become more prevalent and will bring changes to the way people work and play, Scheer maintains, at a minimum, a critical eye should be cast on the rosy visions of the future presented by computer enthusiasts.

One area in which the optimism of computer enthusiasts comes into immediate conflict with the skepticism of critics is education. Those who believe that computers will bring revolutionary changes to society contend that schools should prepare children for that future with computer education. In the opinion of the Consortium for School Networking (CoSN), which advocates providing computers to students and wiring classrooms to networks, education needs to be totally revamped to prepare today's students for a computerized world. In the present system, according to CoSN, teachers are expected to "pour knowledge into students' heads," while students are expected to be passive learners. To function in the future, CoSN asserts, students must become active learners, learning to collaborate and to adapt to changing situations and roles. By giving students access to information through networks and challenging them to collect, analyze, and organize that information, CoSN believes, computers help students to become active learners. Through computerized education, CoSN states, students "acquire skills and attitudes that they will need as information-age workers."

But critics dispute the need for networked computers in schools, contending that computers may actually hamper real learning. According to Clifford Stoll, author of *Silicon Snake Oil: Second Thoughts on the Information Highway,* education requires interaction between good teachers and motivated students, and computers get in the way of this relationship. If students merely gather information from computer networks, in his opinion, they will miss the context and connections that only an experienced teacher can show them. Teachers inspire and educate students in methods of creative problem solving in a way that computers cannot, Stoll contends. He argues that classroom time spent on computers detracts from the real learning that occurs when teachers and students interact. Stoll concludes that it is more important to teach analytical thinking and creativity than computer skills, even if computers are becoming prevalent throughout society.

As computers become ubiquitous and more powerful, their impacts on education, society, personal lives, and business will continue to be watched and debated. The viewpoints included in *Computers and Society: Current Controversies* present a range of views exploring the beneficial and harmful ways that computers may affect individuals and society.

Chapter 1

How Will Computers Transform Society?

Computers and Society: An Overview

by Joel L. Swerdlow

About the author: *Joel L. Swerdlow is a senior writer for* National Geographic.

In Ray Bradbury's *Fahrenheit 451*—which was written in the early 1950s, just after televisions and computers first appeared—people relate most intimately with electronic screens and don't like to read. They are happy when firemen burn books.

Cram people "full of noncombustible data," the fire captain explains. "Chock them so damned full of 'facts' they feel stuffed, but absolutely 'brilliant' with information. Then they'll feel they're thinking, they'll get a *sense* of motion without moving."

The Information Revolution Is Here

Bradbury's novel no longer seems set in a distant future. Thanks to growth in computer capacity, television and computers are merging into digital streams of sounds, images, and text that make it possible to become absolutely brilliant with information.

To know where information technologies are taking us is impossible. The law of unintended consequences governs all technological revolutions. In 1438 Johannes Gutenberg wanted a cheaper way to produce handwritten Bibles. His movable type fostered a spread in literacy, an advance of scientific knowledge, and the emergence of the industrial revolution.

Although no one can predict the full effect of the current information revolution, we can see changes in our daily lives. Look in any classroom. Today's teachers know they have to make lessons fast-moving and entertaining for children raised on television and computer games. Rick Wormeli, an award-winning middle-school teacher in Fairfax County, Virginia, tries to capture the attention of his students by sometimes dressing in yellow shorts, a cape, and red tights and calling himself "Adverb Man." Once, to jump-start the day, he appeared in scuba gear and drenched himself in water. "I try to be as vivid as I can, combining style with substance," he says.

Often the changes that accompany new information technologies are so subtle we barely notice them. Before the written word, people relied on their memories. Before telephones, more people knew the pleasure of writing and receiving letters, the small joy of finding a handwritten envelope in the mailbox from a friend or a relative. Before television and computers, people had a stronger sense of community, a greater attachment to neighborhoods and families.

> ***"To know where information technologies are taking us is impossible."***

Television has glued us to our homes, isolating us from other human beings. Only one-quarter of all Americans know their next-door neighbors. Our communities will become less intimate and more isolated as we earn college credits, begin romances, and gossip on the Internet, a worldwide system that allows computers to communicate with one another. The Age of Software will offer more games, home banking, electronic shopping, video on demand, and a host of other services that unplug us from physical contact.

The decline of human-to-human contact is apparent around the world. Throughout the Middle East, café life—where people used to tell stories over a cup of tea—is disappearing. Bistros are going out of business in Paris; many close earlier in the day. Henri Miquel, owner of Le Dufrénoy, shuts down at 8 p.m. instead of midnight. Where do patrons go? "They rush off to watch television," he says.

Is meeting face-to-face more valuable than corresponding electronically? Some neighbors still stop by when a family crisis strikes, but other people offer condolences via e-mail, written messages transmitted between computers. Whichever we prefer, the electronic seems to represent the future. Television teaches many of us to favor the image over the actual. The Internet pushes life beyond the old physical barriers of time and space. Here you can roam around the world without leaving home. Make new friends. Communicate with astronauts as they circle the earth. Exchange the results of laboratory experiments with a colleague overseas. Read stock quotes. Buy clothes. Research a term paper. Stay out of the office, conducting business via a computer that becomes your virtual office. Virtual community. Virtual travel. Virtual love. A new reality.

Computers Can Foster Human Contact

William Gibson, whose 1984 novel, *Neuromancer*, pioneered the notion of virtual living, now says that electronic communication provides a "sensory expansion for the species by allowing people to experience an extraordinary array of things while staying geographically in the same spot." Gibson warns, however, that the virtual can only augment our physical reality, never replace it. He applauds the countermovement toward what has been called skin—shorthand for contact with other humans.

People who correspond with each other electronically often feel the need for skin and try to meet in what they call real life. Karen Meisner, while an undergraduate at Connecticut's Wesleyan University, was playing a computer game on the Internet in early 1991. During the game she met Pär Winzell, a student at Sweden's Linköping Institute of Technology. He knew her by her game name, Velvet. They began to exchange electronic messages outside the game, sharing thoughts with more directness and intensity than would have been possible in the early stages of a "real-life" relationship. Karen knew something special was happening; they discussed meeting each other. It seemed scary. Then Karen sent an e-mail: "I'm coming to meet you." They have been married for two years.

Technology can also foster skin contact between those who live near one another. Senior citizens in Blacksburg, Virginia, use their computers not only to chat but also to organize get-togethers. "It's like wandering into the town center to meet friends and to check the bulletin board," says Dennis Gentry, a retired Army officer. "Only you can do it in pajamas anytime you want."

The desire for skin can be seen in downtowns and shopping malls—people want human contact even when they could buy things via television or the telephone. Although computers and fax machines make it easier to work at home, business districts continue to grow. More people than ever crowd into major cities, in large part because companies that provide goods and services benefit from being near one another. Employees also seek the relationships that come only from being with other people.

> ***"Before television and computers, people had a stronger sense of community, a greater attachment to neighborhoods and families."***

Need for skin does not negate the electronic screen's power to mesmerize. No brain scan or biochemical study has identified a physical basis for our seemingly insatiable hunger for electronic stimulation. Computers are often more alluring than television, which already has a grip on us. Young Americans today spend about as much time in front of a television as in a classroom. At midnight 1.8 million children under age 12 are still watching television. The average adult American watches more than 30 hours every week.

Parents could restrict their children's electronic consumption. But we, too, are addicted. Give up electronic links for a day? No telephone, television, or computer? Try a week. Few can do it. Momentum is in the opposite direction. When a two-year-old clicks at the keyboard and the next day says, "Mommy, Daddy, more 'puter," his parents feel something good is happening.

Dependence on Electronic Devices May Increase

Our dependency on the "electronic needle" will increase if wireless, palm-size receivers become available. These devices—a combination telephone, computer, fax, and television—will provide hundreds of video, audio, and text channels. Handheld receivers that link to e-mail, Internet services, and fax communications are already on the market, but too expensive for most people. Such technological innovations do not permeate a society until someone can profit from them. The first fax was sent from Lyon to Paris in 1865, but use of faxes did not become widespread until technology made text encoding and transmission much cheaper, 120 years later.

> ***"People who correspond with each other electronically often . . . try to meet in what they call real life."***

Reliance on the electronic screen is part of something larger, the spread of technological civilization. George Steiner, a cultural historian who teaches at Cambridge University, warns that this civilization produces a creeping sameness that threatens local cultures.

The source of most of this uniformity is the advertising and entertainment industries. Worldwide sales of American movies and television programs now total more than five billion dollars a year. A New Delhi newspaper calls these media "termites eating away at our traditional values."

But human nature resists the sameness that comes with electronic communication. The place in which we live—its resources and history—maintains a tremendous pull on us, even when we are not conscious of it. When told we are the same, we turn to geographic roots and tribal groupings to find a sense of belonging. This helps explain why ethnic loyalties enjoy a resurgence even as individuals bind themselves to the electronic screen. Such resistance may prevent the apocalyptic *Fahrenheit 451* from emerging, but as the novel predicts, information technologies threaten the book.

Stakes are high. From texts written on papyrus 4,000 years ago through today, books have provided memory and depth. Until the current electronic challenge, they have been the central vehicle through which most societies have perceived themselves. Perhaps that is why Bill Gates, chairman of the Microsoft Corporation and computer guru, arranged to have his account of the information revolution published the old-fashioned way—on paper, between hard covers. Of all the issues associated with the information explosion—such as privacy, copyright, libel, and computer theft—the battle of the book may have the greatest impact.

Computers and the Future of Books

At first glance books are in good shape. Sales in the U.S. are the highest ever. Chains of huge bookstores—many offering 150,000 titles—are prospering. Technology, furthermore, encourages reliance on the written word. Tens of billions of words pass through the Internet daily. The ease of printing and photocopying digital information has raised paper usage to record levels.

But TV and computers spawn aliteracy among many people, who are unwilling to read anything of substantive length requiring concentration. Brevity.

Five-second sound bites. Channel surfing. Instant gratification. Fast-moving images. Constant stimulation. Shorter attention spans. A world in which the worst sin is to be boring.

Books are taking on new forms, relying on technological zip, which makes the traditional book look like a horse and buggy. This appeals to the new expectations of readers. Interactive multimedia books offer seamless sequences of sounds, images, and words. Learning a foreign language? Listen to spoken pronunciation as you read. Studying algebra? See equations move across an electronic chalkboard. Want to learn more about a specific word in the text? Click on it and explanations fill your screen.

Sales of electronic encyclopedias exceed sales of printed ones. Electronic dominance over print will increase if "netbooks," which could provide wireless connections to libraries, become available. Flip one on and read whatever you want wherever you are. Netbooks will never become popular, however, without improvements in screen technology. On-screen reading is currently 20 to 30 percent slower—and much less comfortable—than print reading because of glare, flickering images, and other problems.

Although people love today's print-on-paper books, those who resist new technology can be left behind. In the early 1500s, nearly a century after Gutenberg's movable type, many people continued to believe that value and beauty came only from handwritten manuscripts. These laboriously crafted works have an artistic appeal that printed books cannot match. Federigo da Montefeltro, a leader of the Italian Renaissance, said he "would have been ashamed to own a printed book." Such attitudes isolated people from new ideas and scientific information that were available only in printed format.

New Types of Books Inspired by Computers

Technological changes in books are part of a larger change in our aesthetic sensibilities and creativity. Video images and computer screens appear in plays and operas. Choreography and architecture rely on computer programs.

The novel, which began as epic poems in Homer's era, will also evolve. In an Internet story every reader can add new material. The traditional notion of "author" and "original," which arrived when written books replaced oral folklore, disappears. At Brown University, students in the Hypertext Fiction Workshop listen to John Coltrane and study how Matisse perceived space. They are learning how to integrate sound and visuals into stories.

> ***"Reliance on the electronic screen is part of something larger, the spread of technological civilization."***

Novelist Robert Coover, who teaches the workshop, decries "the tyranny of the line." He lauds the "hypertext novel," in which a story has no predetermined beginning, middle, or end. Readers choose among pathways within plots that form a mosaic. Although only 10,000 or so of these novels sold in the U.S. in 1994, sales have increased 40 percent since 1993. Bob Arellano, one of Coover's former students, recently completed *@Itamont*, an electronic novel soon to be available on CD-ROM. The novel offers two beginnings. Those who click on "Innocence" read about a young couple's first kiss; those who choose "Experience" read about a murder. Both stories then weave in and out of the same narrative territory. Neither has a given middle or end. The readers, in Arellano's words, "walk through story space in their own way."

> ***"Of all the issues associated with the information explosion . . . the battle of the book may have the greatest impact."***

Young people may find mosaic plots exciting, but for those schooled to think in a linear fashion, hypertext novels can be tedious and confusing. No hypertext novel can achieve what the brain does naturally. In Fyodor Dostoyevsky's *Crime and Punishment*, Raskolnikov sees a pretty young woman on the street. He walks toward her. Her skirt is torn. As he gets closer, he sees that her face is flushed and swollen. Readers react to this timeless passage in different ways, creating their own combinations of texture, mood, detail, and emotion. We do this effortlessly.

Information technologies, for all the attention they receive, lag far behind the power of the human brain. Researchers estimate that the normal brain has a quadrillion connections between its nerve cells, more than all the phone calls made in the U.S. in the past decade.

Computers and the International Economy

But human power is becoming increasingly ineffective in controlling the way information technology shapes our economic and political lives. Geographic location of resources, labor, and capital means less as scattered countries use information technologies to work together. Many cars have parts made in a half dozen countries; stores sell look-alike clothes sewn on four continents. The reason? Management can control quality and coordinate production without regard to place or distance. Money moves most easily. Stocks, currency, and bonds traded on worldwide electronic markets amount to an estimated three trillion dollars each day, twice the annual U.S. budget.

Two generations ago, political analysts gauged global economic relationships by counting movements of railcars between countries. Now they count traffic on telecommunications networks. What they are discovering is unexpected. According to studies by Gregory Staple, a communications lawyer in Washington, D.C., Canada made more calls to Hong Kong than to France in 1993. A third of India's traffic went to Arab nations.

Speed of information transmission did not create this international economy. Lowering of costs did. Instantaneous international communication has existed for more than a century. In 1872, when Jules Verne's fictional Phileas Fogg was trying to travel around the world in 80 days, a telegram from the detective chasing him traveled the globe in minutes. But until recently, international wires were used only by economic and political elites. A 1965 transatlantic cable could carry 130 simultaneous conversations. Today's fiber-optic cable can carry more than 500,000, dramatically lowering costs.

A growing number of workers in this info-environment must be able to absorb, manipulate, and market information. Peter Drucker, a management expert whose ideas have influenced the world's largest corporations, estimates that by the year 2000 such work will be the primary task of at least a third of the U.S. workforce.

This information economy favors small entrepreneurial ventures that can quickly adapt to new technologies. This is why, to cite a phenomenon evident in American cities, an estimated two-thirds of the private companies in Los Angeles did not exist in 1970. Mike Forti, an L.A. businessman, has sales pending for more than 30 million dollars' worth of American equipment to Gazprom, Russia's gas company. He makes all his deals via fax, telephone, and e-mail from his home. He rarely meets his colleagues.

Yet Forti's business began with old-fashioned friendship. While he was studying how to participate in the world economy, a friend asked Forti if he was interested in doing business with his brother-in-law's firm in Moscow. Forti's next venture, arranged through other friends, involves selling equipment in India. The power of skin created the opportunity for a business conducted electronically.

Information Technology and Politics

To stay competitive in this international economy, a country must open itself to information and ideas. Government attempts to control information—Romania even tried to restrict the use of typewriters—inevitably fail, not only because of economic pressures but also because technology continually assaults authority. Satellite broadcasts saturate Iran with *Charlie's Angels* and other forbidden programs. Rebels in the jungles of Mexico's Chiapas state post statements on the Internet. The Indonesian government bans the work of Pramoedya Ananta Toer, whose novels are acclaimed throughout the world, but Indonesians can flip on their computers and print out his writing.

> ***"Technological changes in books are part of a larger change in our aesthetic sensibilities and creativity."***

A lesson in the power of information comes from China and Burma, whose soldiers killed thousands of demonstrators in the late 1980s. The soldiers obeyed orders. But their governments reportedly isolated select units of soldiers and told them elaborate lies to keep them from knowing the demonstrators' pro-democracy goals. One

Burmese student who escaped such killings in September 1988 later chatted with an army private. "I had no idea," the soldier said. "I thought you were communists and foreigners trying to take over the country."

"Geographic location of resources, labor, and capital means less as scattered countries use information technologies to work together."

Some governments, particularly in the developing world, try to mix economic openness with authoritarian politics. They may enjoy temporary success. But in the long run—as Taiwan, Chile, and others demonstrate—free-flowing information nurtures democracy.

At the same time, massive amounts of information are changing democracy itself. Personality and publicity have superseded political parties. Issues must be presented quickly, with visual aids. Important problems, such as the relationship between unemployment and crime, rarely capture public attention. We want more than the news; we want the new news, things that are new since we last heard the news. Government officials, academic experts, and other leaders have less of a monopoly on information. Public opinion plays a larger role in public policy and diplomacy.

Information Technology Affects Public Policy

The availability of information can have an immediate impact. You can call the Right-to-Know-Network by dialing 202-234-8570 on a modem, register for a free account, and then instantly find out which of some 300 toxic chemicals have been emitted in your area. This information had been buried within regulatory bureaucracies but now stimulates lawsuits, local action, and government responsiveness. Kathy Grandfield, a paralegal in Sedalia, Missouri, wondered whether a nearby chemical plant caused her family's flu-like illnesses and the death of birds in her yard. She discovered from Right-to-Know that chemical emissions may have been a contributing cause. She and her neighbors—who also had similar symptoms for years—worked together to help clean up the plant.

Will those who master these tools unfairly influence public policymaking? And who will control access to extraordinary new bandwidths that allow information to travel faster and cheaper to more people? The Internet grew out of a Defense Department communications system designed in the 1960s to survive nuclear war. Because such rationales no longer exist, marketplace forces have replaced government funding. The Internet could become advertiser driven like broadcast TV and radio, but no one knows how this would affect the accessibility and content of services.

High costs are splitting us into information haves and have-nots, thereby threatening democratic principles. Countries, too, are being divided into haves and have-nots. In many developing nations, a majority of people have no telephones or computers. Even if they did, their machines would be idle unless governments were able to invest billions of dollars in telecommunications infrastructure—primarily cables, satellites, and transmitters. And this would not bridge the gap—a third of all people in developing nations cannot read.

No One Knows the Future of Computers

Some of us will cross into the new world; others will remain behind. New worlders will pull even further ahead as technologies evolve, possibly even computers that mimic human reasoning and sensory perception. No one knows what kind of network will succeed the Internet, or what increasing computer power will make possible. We may eventually rely on digital navigation genies who sort through junk and decipher messages. One trend is clear: A growing cultlike faith in information, a belief that if we hook up to the Internet we'll be smart. Full of facts. Brilliant with information. Sense of motion without moving. It's right out of *Fahrenheit 451*.

> ***"In the long run . . . free-flowing information nurtures democracy."***

Technology promises more and more information for less and less effort. As we hear these promises, we must balance faith in technology with faith in ourselves. Wisdom and insight often come not from keeping up-to-date or compiling facts but from quiet reflection. What we hold most valuable—things like morality and compassion—can be found only within us. While embracing the future, we can remain loyal to our unchanging humanity.

Computers Will Significantly Transform Society

by Nicholas Negroponte

About the author: *Nicholas Negroponte, who writes a monthly column for* Wired, *a magazine about developments in computer technology and popular culture, is the director of the Massachusetts Institute of Technology's Media Lab. He is also the author of* Being Digital, *from which this viewpoint is excerpted.*

Being dyslexic, I don't like to read. As a child I read train timetables instead of the classics, and delighted in making imaginary perfect connections from one obscure town in Europe to another. This fascination gave me an excellent grasp of European geography.

Thirty years later, as director of the MIT Media Lab, I found myself in the middle of a heated national debate about the transfer of technology from U.S. research universities to foreign companies. I was soon summoned to two industry-government meetings, one in Florida and one in California.

Exchange of Goods vs. Exchange of Information

At both meetings, Evian water was served in one-liter glass bottles. Unlike most of the participants, I knew exactly where Evian was from my timetables. Evian, France, is more than five hundred miles from the Atlantic Ocean. Those heavy glass bottles had to traverse almost one-third of Europe, cross the Atlantic, and, in the case of California, travel an additional three thousand miles.

So here we were discussing the protection of the American computer industry and our electronic competitiveness, when we seemingly could not even provide American water at an American conference.

Today, I see my Evian story not so much being about French mineral water versus American, but illustrating the fundamental difference between atoms and bits. World trade has traditionally consisted of exchanging atoms. In the case of

Evian water, we were shipping a large, heavy, and inert mass, slowly, painfully, and expensively, across thousands of miles, over a period of many days. When you go through customs you declare your atoms, not your bits. Even digitally recorded music is distributed on plastic CDs, with huge packaging, shipping, and inventory costs.

This is changing rapidly. The methodical movement of recorded music as pieces of plastic, like the slow human handling of most information in the form of books, magazines, newspapers, and videocassettes, is about to become the instantaneous and inexpensive transfer of electronic data that move at the speed of light. In this form, the information can become universally accessible. Thomas Jefferson advanced the concept of libraries and the right to check out a book free of charge. But this great forefather never considered the likelihood that 20 million people might access a digital library electronically and withdraw its contents at no cost.

The change from atoms to bits is irrevocable and unstoppable.

The Exponential Growth of Computer Use

Why now? Because the change is also exponential—small differences of yesterday can have suddenly shocking consequences tomorrow.

Did you ever know the childhood conundrum of working for a penny a day for a month, but doubling your salary each day? If you started this wonderful pay scheme on New Year's Day, you would be earning more than $10 million per day on the last day of January. This is the part most people remember. What we do not realize is that, using the same scheme, we would earn only about $1.3 million if January were three days shorter (i.e., February). Put another way, your cumulative income for that whole month of February would be roughly $2.6 million, instead of the $21 million you earned in total during January. When an effect is exponential, those last three days mean a lot! We are approaching those last three days in the spread of computing and digital telecommunications.

In the same exponential fashion, computers are moving into our daily lives: 35 percent of American families and 50 percent of American teenagers have a personal computer at home; 30 million people are estimated to be on the Internet; 65 percent of new computers sold worldwide in 1994 were for the home; and 90 percent of those to be sold in 1995 are expected to have modems or CD-ROM drives. These numbers do not even include the fifty microprocessors in the average 1995 automobile, or the microprocessors in your toaster, thermostat, answering machine, CD player, and greeting cards. And if I am wrong about any of the numbers above, just wait a minute.

"The change from atoms to bits is irrevocable and unstoppable."

And the rate at which these numbers are growing is astonishing. The use of one computer program, a browser for the Internet called Mosaic, grew 11 percent per week between February and December 1993. The population of the Internet itself is now increasing at 10 percent per month. If this rate of growth were to continue (quite impossibly), the total number of Internet users would exceed the population of the world by 2003.

> ***"Computing is not about computers any more. It is about living."***

Some people worry about the social divide between the information-rich and the information-poor, the haves and the have-nots, the First and the Third Worlds. But the real cultural divide is going to be generational. When I meet an adult who tells me he has discovered CD-ROM, I can guess that he has a child between five and ten years old. When I meet someone who tells me she has discovered America Online, there is probably a teenager in her house. One is an electronic book, the other a socializing medium. Both are being taken for granted by children the same way adults don't think about air (until it is missing).

Computers in the Future

Computing is not about computers any more. It is about living. The giant central computer, the so-called mainframe, has been almost universally replaced by personal computers. We have seen computers move out of giant air-conditioned rooms into closets, then onto desktops, and now into our laps and pockets. But this is not the end.

Early in the next millennium your right and left cuff links or earrings may communicate with each other by low-orbiting satellites and have more computer power than your present PC. Your telephone won't ring indiscriminately; it will receive, sort, and perhaps respond to your incoming calls like a well-trained English butler. Mass media will be redefined by systems for transmitting and receiving personalized information and entertainment. Schools will change to become more like museums and playgrounds for children to assemble ideas and socialize with other children all over the world. The digital planet will look and feel like the head of a pin.

As we interconnect ourselves, many of the values of a nation-state will give way to those of both larger and smaller electronic communities. We will socialize in digital neighborhoods in which physical space will be irrelevant and time will play a different role. Twenty years from now, when you look out a window, what you see may be five thousand miles and six time zones away. When you watch an hour of television, it may have been delivered to your home in less than a second. Reading about Patagonia can include the sensory experience of going there. A book by William Buckley can be a conversation with him.

Personal Computers Will Transform the Home

by Eckhard Pfeiffer

About the author: *Eckhard Pfeiffer is president and CEO of Compaq Computer Corporation.*

Today's PC has evolved to the point of fundamentally redefining experience for people of all ages.

In fact, the PC has progressed so far and so fast along the inventive continuum that it now defines the computer industry. And it will come to define the consumer electronics industry as well.

The Evolution and Growth of Computer Use

As computing and communications have fused, we've seen the PC evolve from a stand-alone personal productivity device to a communications tool—a connector and coordinator. And when combined with the Internet, the PC can radically transform personal and business communication, commerce, education, healthcare delivery, home automation, entertainment and play, and perhaps even government.

The PC's life-changing power is not lost on people. While personal computers are in just one-third of American homes today, many, many more people aspire to owning a PC, mostly because of its educational value. A recent survey found that more than 80 percent of people who plan to buy one soon say it's mainly for their children's education. We know that a majority of all computer purchases are influenced by a child in the household.

So by 1998, we expect half of American homes to have at least one PC. In fact, households with more than one computer will become as common as households with more than one TV, VCR, or phone.

According to market researcher Link Resources, 11 million U.S. homes already have two or more working PCs. New users tend to spend more time on the PC than in front of the TV.

Why is this happening?

From Eckhard Pfeiffer, "The PC Platform," the keynote address delivered on January 5, 1996, to the Winter Consumer Electronics Show, Las Vegas, Nevada. Reprinted by permission of the author.

Well, the PC's become so versatile and such a magnet for more and more functionality that the entire family wants to use it at the same time. And who can blame them? Can you think of any other mass market product that has proved so adaptable, so multiform, so elastic in function, definition, and price?

The same PC can be used today as a telephone, a fax machine, a modem, a scanner, copier, and TV. It can be used as a connection to the increasingly commercialized and ubiquitous Internet. It can be used as a node on the office network. A tool for managing personal finance or educating and entertaining children. A vehicle for telecommuting and videoconferencing. A place to play audio and video CD-ROMs. As well as an intelligent command center for controlling your major appliances and monitoring your home's energy use and security systems.

"The PC's become so versatile and such a magnet for more and more functionality that the entire family wants to use it at the same time."

What's more, the PC can connect to nearly every kind of communications infrastructure. You can hook it up to analog and ISDN (integrated switched digital network) lines, to Ethernet, cable, infrared, and wireless communications of all kinds.

And that's essential because people want to connect—to one another, to the Internet, to on-line services, to businesses, to the ocean of information in cyberspace. Little surprise then that in 1995 the two-phone-line household became a common fact of life. The connection machine par excellence is the PC. And this gateway device keeps getting more and more powerful. . . .

Computers in Every Room

I see the PC as a universal tool for home and business. By universal tool I mean it does many things well. And its features, form factor, and price can be tailored to suit the activities that go on in the different rooms of your home. I believe the PC now has a place in nearly every room of your home. And yet it won't be the same kind of computer in each room.

We've put this idea into practice by helping design what we call the Information Highway House. It's a real four-bedroom house located just north of San Francisco in Corte Madera. Inside are five different Compaq PCs linked in an Ethernet-based local area network.

With these PCs, family members can schedule a doctor's appointment, buy stocks, or pay bills electronically from the den. They can research a school project or listen to interactive books from the bedroom. They can look up a recipe on the kitchen PC, and laugh at comedy routines in the living room. This cyberspace house represents just the earliest stages of what will be possible before the turn of the century.

I say that because today's PC has only just entered its adolescence. Its hormones are just kicking in. Its major growth and the realization of its full potential lie ahead. In fact, it's as far from a commodity as a product can be. To know that's true, just consider how many really different versions of the PC are emerging. Everything from high-end clustered multiprocessor servers for the datacenter, to room-specific devices for the home, to lightweight, mobile PC companions that combine data transmission and voice recognition capabilities.

No single commodity motherboard can meet all these form factors or all customer needs cost effectively. I think the PC is about where the automobile was back in the 1920s. While we're past the equivalent of drivers needing to crank and choke their cars by hand, we're not yet to the point of automatic transmission—let alone antilock brakes and air bags. In short, PC advances in the next two decades will dwarf those of the past two.

Now, there are other reasons for my optimism. Given the momentum behind the Internet, we're going to see a major increase in communications bandwidth to the home. This bandwidth will be delivered by ISDN, broadband over copper wires, cable modems, direct digital satellite services, and ultimately all-optical networks.

The Computerized Home of the Future

What's more, we at Compaq are convinced there's enormous opportunity to integrate the PC far more completely into the home. Your home can have far more diverse and interactive links to the outside world. That way you can pull in digital content on demand along with a wealth of information and services. And you can engage in full-blown electronic commerce, telemedicine, and distance learning.

Equally important, I believe your home itself can become a far more intelligent and automated environment and as programmable as a PC.

These developments are pulling us toward the Intelligent Networked Home of the very near future. I know the idea of a "smart home" has been around for decades. Back in the 1950s, science fiction writer Ray Bradbury offered a memorable vision.

In one of his short stories, he described a 21st century house where the front door recognizes visitors and lets them in, the kitchen ceiling "speaks," reminding you which bills are due today. And tiny robot mice roam the floors collecting dust.

> ***"The PC now has a place in nearly every room of your home."***

In another story, we read about a family whose house has a special room built just for the kids. It's a virtual reality nursery that brings to life in three dimensions whatever scene the kids are thinking about, whether it's the cow jumping over a very realistic moon, lions prowling an African plain, or more to the point, parents turning over their car keys and credit cards to their kids.

Compaq's vision of the intelligent home is a bit more down to earth and it's available this century!

Home Computers of the Very Near Future

With that in mind, let's consider the following scenario. Suppose it's January 5th in the year 2000. It's a weekday, 6:30 in the morning. You shuffle to the kitchen in search of coffee and turn on your voice- and touchscreen-activated kitchen PC-TV.

> ***"Your home itself can become a far more intelligent and automated environment and as programmable as a PC."***

With its advanced digital display system, this PC can handle the spectrum of bandwidths, aspect ratios, and scan rates depending on the content you've selected. And it's linked to a multichannel, multipoint distribution system whether wireless digital broadcast, wireless cable, or digital satellite video and data.

You select CNN *Headline News*, which reports that the Winter Consumer Electronics Show is under way. You notice a live satellite feed of CES is available and watch a few minutes of the opening keynote. With a touch of the PC's keypad, you check for any pressing phone, fax, or E-mail messages delivered overnight.

Software agents that act on your behalf by knowing your interests prioritize your messages and point out a conflict in your schedule for the day. These agents interact with you on your monitor through animated facial expressions.

While this is happening, your wife is in the bedroom seated by a large-screen PC connected to wide-area ATM-based, broadband services. She's flying to China this afternoon for an extended business trip. But before leaving the country, she wants to consult with her doctor to make sure her vaccinations are up to date.

While waiting for her scheduled 7:00 a.m. telemedicine appointment, she reads her personalized electronic newspaper, which was compiled overnight by her software agents scanning the network. This morning's lead stories notify her of a delay in her flight's departure, Beijing restaurant reviews, and an acquisition just undertaken by the Chinese customer she's visiting. . . .

At 7:00 sharp a chime sounds, and her doctor's face appears in a high-quality video tile on her PC. She touches the tile with her finger, causing it to fill the screen. During this personal videoconference, her doctor reviews her medical record and the latest health advisories from China.

Meanwhile, your teenage daughter starts her day as she always does, by jumping on the I-phone (the Internet phone) to talk to a friend in Germany. She also logs into a video rental store on the Net, looks at a dozen movie trailers, and selects the one she'll watch that evening on the living room PC-TV, which has a 60-inch screen. . . .

After your wife leaves for the airport, and the kids head off to day care and school, you drive to the office for a quick meeting. Your house, sensing it's now empty, automatically switches to "away mode," turning off lights, closing drapes, dialing back the thermostat, and resetting the security system. In fact, your home network is constantly monitoring its subsystems, ready to page you if there's any change from the normal settings.

Later that morning while you're at work, your home security system sends you an urgent page with the message: "Front window broken. Security company called." With voice commands directed at your desktop PC, you dial into your home remotely. You speak your personal ID code and then say: "Activate control console. Activate security camera."

You take a quick pan of your front yard and notice a tree limb leaning against your house, and a crack running the length of your living room window. Relieved that no one has broken in, you send an "all-clear" signal to your security company. And then you say to your computer: "Find a nearby glass repair service and dial the number."

Two hours later, a technician from "Window Doktor" arrives in your driveway. Your security system senses someone approaching your front door and pages you again. The technician holds his badge up to the security camera for verification, and you remotely unlock the front door.

A couple of hours later, he sends a page that the window has been replaced and the bill comes to $485. And over the Web, you send a secure electronic payment to "WindowDoktor.com."

When you get home that evening, you decide to call up the energy management program on your PC. This gives you an up-to-the-minute look at your phone and utility bills. It also lets you save money by shifting your peak power consumption to times of day when rates are significantly lower.

"With a touch of the PC's keypad, you check for any pressing phone, fax, or E-mail messages delivered overnight."

Now I could continue with this scenario, but you get a sense of the wealth of convenience offered by an intelligent Networked Home. Perhaps you're thinking if this is not complete fantasy, then it must require the resources of a Warren Buffett [as of 1995, the wealthiest man in America]. Well, we believe this scenario is not only feasible but affordable. Most of the technology needed to fully implement home automation and provide valuable services is here today. . . .

Through the centuries, the focal point of the house has changed several times. Early on, it was the fireplace. People gathered around it to keep warm and cook their meals. Over time, that focal point switched to the kitchen. And then it seemed to switch to the TV. But now, I believe the home's new focal point is becoming the PC.

Computers Will Not Significantly Transform Society

by Clifford Stoll

About the author: *Clifford Stoll is the author of* Silicon Snake Oil: Second Thoughts on the Information Highway.

After two decades online, I'm perplexed. It's not that I haven't had a gas of a good time on the Internet. I've met great people and even caught a hacker or two. But today I'm uneasy about this most trendy and oversold community. Visionaries see a future of telecommuting workers, interactive libraries and multimedia classrooms. They speak of electronic town meetings and virtual communities. Commerce and business will shift from offices and malls to networks and modems. And the freedom of digital networks will make government more democratic.

Computer Hype vs. Reality

Baloney. Do our computer pundits lack all common sense? The truth is no online database will replace your daily newspaper, no CD-ROM can take the place of a competent teacher and no computer network will change the way government works.

Consider today's online world. The Usenet, a worldwide bulletin board, allows anyone to post messages across the nation. Your word gets out, leapfrogging editors and publishers. Every voice can be heard cheaply and instantly. The result? Every voice is heard. The cacophony more closely resembles citizens band radio, complete with handles, harassment and anonymous threats. When most everyone shouts, few listen. How about electronic publishing? Try reading a book on disc. At best, it's an unpleasant chore: the myopic glow of a clunky computer replaces the friendly pages of a book. And you can't tote that laptop to the beach. Yet Nicholas Negroponte, director of the MIT Media Lab,

From Clifford Stoll, "The Internet? Bah!" *Newsweek*, February 27, 1995.

predicts that we'll soon buy books and newspapers straight over the Internet. Uh, sure.

What the Internet hucksters won't tell you is that the Internet is an ocean of unedited data, without any pretense of completeness. Lacking editors, reviewers or critics, the Internet has become a wasteland of unfiltered data. You don't know what to ignore and what's worth reading. Logged onto the World Wide Web, I hunt for the date of the Battle of Trafalgar. Hundreds of files show up, and it takes 15 minutes to unravel them—one's a biography written by an eighth grader, the second is a computer game that doesn't work and the third is an image of a London monument. None answers my question, and my search is periodically interrupted by messages like, "Too many connections, try again later."

"The Internet is an ocean of unedited data, without any pretense of completeness."

Won't the Internet be useful in governing? Internet addicts clamor for government reports. But when Andy Spano ran for county executive in Westchester County, N.Y., he put every press release and position paper onto a bulletin board. In that affluent county with plenty of computer companies, how many voters logged in? Fewer than 30. Not a good omen.

Computers and Education

Point and click: Then there are those pushing computers into schools. We're told that multimedia will make schoolwork easy and fun. Students will happily learn from animated characters while taught by expertly tailored software. Who needs teachers when you've got computer-aided education? Bah. These expensive toys are difficult to use in classrooms and require extensive teacher training. Sure, kids love videogames—but think of your own experience: can you recall even one educational filmstrip of decades past? I'll bet you remember the two or three great teachers who made a difference in your life.

Then there's cyberbusiness. We're promised instant catalog shopping—just point and click for great deals. We'll order airline tickets over the network, make restaurant reservations and negotiate sales contracts. Stores will become obsolete. So how come my local mall does more business in an afternoon than the entire Internet handles in a month? Even if there were a trustworthy way to send money over the Internet—which there isn't—the network is missing a most essential ingredient of capitalism: salespeople.

Computers Lack the Human Touch

What's missing from this electronic wonderland? Human contact. Discount the fawning technoburble about virtual communities. Computers and networks isolate us from one another. A network chat line is a limp substitute for meeting friends over coffee. No interactive multimedia display comes close to the excitement of a live concert. And who'd prefer cybersex to the real thing? While the Internet beckons brightly, seductively flashing an icon of knowledge-as-power, this nonplace lures us to surrender our time on earth. A poor substitute it is, this virtual reality where frustration is legion and where—in the holy names of Education and Progress—important aspects of human interactions are relentlessly devalued.

Future Societal Transformations Cannot Be Predicted

by Jay Ambrose

About the author: *Jay Ambrose is a chief editorial writer and syndicated columnist for Scripps Howard News Service.*

If the approaching new year has prompted you to think about the new century and millennium that reside just around the corner, and if you have been experiencing some trepidation about what lies in the future, just trot down to the bookstore for a copy of *The Road Ahead.*

It's about the information superhighway, it's by Bill Gates and it's a sermon in techno-uplift. Before you can say silicon, this book should have you whistling a cheerful tune.

Unwarranted Enthusiasm for the Information Highway

No brave new world has ever been so adoringly embraced as the information superhighway is by Mr. Gates. Evincing an unblinking enthusiasm, he predicts the new technology will enhance leisure time, enrich culture, cure urban problems, protect the environment, spur the economy, improve education and—if he doesn't quite say it, he surely comes close—deliver something akin to universal happiness.

His is an anticipatory ecstasy most careful thinkers are not going to share, but Mr. Gates will still be taken seriously for the same reason many people get taken seriously in this land: He is rich, not just a little rich, but $15 billion rich, ahead of perhaps everyone on the planet except some Saudi prince who had his wealth handed to him.

Mr. Gates earned his wealth through skillful entrepreneurship, but it was nothing so pedestrian as money that propelled him to hang around computers as a teen-ager or to drop out of Harvard and go into the software business.

From Jay Ambrose, "Superhighway to Infinite Happiness?" *Washington Times*, December 31, 1995. Reprinted by permission of the Scripps Howard News Service, a division of United Media.

What tickled his fancy was this incredible trick with binary numbers that allows electronic machines to store and transmit unimagineable gobs of information.

Computers, Mr. Gates says in his book, are now inexpensive and all around us, and they're going to join together to form a network to allow all of us to communicate easily with each other.

That's it; that's the essence of the information superhighway, something far outreaching the Internet. It's every person and group hooked up to every other person and group.

It can come about, says Mr. Gates, only when an objective adopted by his company is realized: "A computer on every desk and in every home."

Bill Gates's New Uses for Computers

His company is Microsoft, which he wants to help lead us to that day "when you will be able to conduct business, study, explore the world and its cultures, call up any great entertainment, make friends, attend neighborhood markets and show pictures to distant relatives without leaving your desk or armchair."

What a picture our hero paints!

"You will be able to stay in touch with anyone, anywhere, who wants to stay in touch with you; to browse through any of thousands of libraries, day or night."

Mr. Gates thinks there will be a "wallet PC" that will shop for you, buy tickets, be a substitute for cash, provide all sorts of on-scene information and do just about everything but make love, although even here Mr. Gates has a computer answer, something you've already heard of, something called "virtual reality."

The Concept of Virtual Reality

Virtual reality is a simulation so close to reality that you maybe don't need reality.

It's easy enough, Mr. Gates says, to create the necessary sound (headphones) and sight (goggles). Creating the other sensory experiences will require a body-suit with tiny sensor-feedback devices that will be in contact with your nose, mouth and the complete surface of your skin.

> ***"No one—not Mr. Gates, not me, not you—can predict all the ways in which computer technology will be used or affect society."***

Many questions have been asked about virtual sex, Mr. Gates acknowledges, and he says, yeah, that will happen, but it eventually won't be as important as other stuff.

Hmmm.

Most of what Mr. Gates defines as the information superhighway won't begin happening, in his view, for another decade. The cost in the United States alone could be $120 billion, although no one has quite figured out yet how to recoup that kind of investment.

Mr. Gates concedes many difficulties and is smart enough to recognize that his prognostications could make him look silly in years to come. But he remains optimistic to the point of giddiness.

The Questionable Benefits of Other Technological Innovations

To begin to see where maybe he's mistaken, consider that television has been a society-shaking technology for about 40 years now. In TV's early days, enthusiasts forecast how it would educate Americans and bring opera and Shakespeare into every living room. In 1939, David Sarnoff, CEO of RCA, said: "It is probable that television drama of high caliber and produced by first-rate artists will materially raise the level of dramatic taste of the nation."

The last time I checked, the level had been raised to Beavis and Butthead.

No one—not Mr. Gates, not me, not you—can predict all the ways in which computer technology will be used or affect society.

> ***"Any technology is just a tool, and tools can be used for good or evil."***

In his book *Technopoly*, Neil Postman provides historical examples of the utterly unforeseeable consequences of technology.

Mechanical clocks originated in Benedictine monasteries to provide regularity in the day's devotions. Ultimately, they synchronized and controlled work, making capitalism possible.

Johannes Gutenberg, inventor of the printing press, was a devout Roman Catholic. He could never have anticipated a mass-produced Bible would "make each Christian his own theologian"—and thus lead to Protestantism.

Computers Are Simply Tools

It's thrilling to Mr. Gates that computers could make it possible for people to carry out practically every errand and work-related duty from their homes. He says people will still socialize because they are social animals and, after all, TV has not kept people from socializing.

In fact, some data demonstrate that TV probably has reduced the hours people spend in the sorts of voluntary organizations that are crucial for the functioning of a democratic society.

Any technology is just a tool, and tools can be used for good or evil. Perhaps the Internet has facilitated as much intellectual exchange as letter-writing (though I doubt it), but it has also facilitated the distribution of pornography.

Thoreau once said machines are just improved means to unimproved ends, and another writer, Raymond D. Fosdick, summed up the issue well in a book in 1928, *The Old Savage in a New Civilization*. He noted that science actually increases mankind's destructive ability without conferring any comparable growth in moral judgment.

"Knowledge may mean power, but it does not necessarily mean capacity.

Modern science has revolutionized, not man, but his world."

I'm not arguing that some slippery slide down the information superhighway will be the end of civilization as we know it. I'm actually grateful to computers. For 30 years, I've earned my living in association with newspapers, which might not be around today in recognizable form if high-tech had not made it possible to decrease labor costs at a time revenue was shrinking.

But neither do I think the information superhighway is the road to human happiness that the Gates book suggests it will be.

Computers Will Create Unemployment

by David Noble

About the author: *David Noble is a professor of history at York University in North York, Ontario, Canada. He is the author of* Progress Without People: New Technology, Unemployment, and the Message of Resistance.

At the end of November 1994, the truth about the information highway finally got out. Protesting the announcement of another 5,600 layoffs, 1,200 Bell-Atlantic employees in Pennsylvania wore T-shirts to work which graphically depicted themselves as Information Highway Roadkill. The layoffs were just the latest round of cutbacks at Bell-Atlantic, which have been matched by the elimination of jobs at the other giants of the telecommunications industry—ATT, NYNEX, Northern Telecom—supposedly the very places where new jobs are to be created with the information highway. In reality, the technology is enabling companies to extend their operations and enlarge their profits while reducing their workforce and the pay and security of those who remain by contracting out work to cheaper labor around the globe and by replacing people with machines. The very workers who are constructing the new information infrastructure are among the first to go, but not the only ones. The same fate is facing countless workers in manufacturing and service industries in the wake of the introduction of these new information technologies.

Information Highway Roadkill

What is most striking about the Bell-Atlantic episode is not just the provocative fashion statement of the workers, members of Communication Workers of America District 13. Rather, it was the company's exaggerated response. Bell-Atlantic demanded that the workers remove the T-shirts and, when they refused, it suspended them without pay. According to Vince Maison, president of the union, the employer suspended the employees out of expressed fear that their message would be seen by the public. Significantly, management was concerned about adverse publicity not just for Bell-Atlantic but, more importantly,

From David Noble, "The Truth About the Information Highway," *Monthly Review*, June 1995.

for the information highway itself. This was the first time the information highway was unambiguously linked with unemployment, by a union and workforce presumably best situated to reap its promised benefits. Apparently the company believed there was too much riding on the information highway bandwagon to allow this sober message to get around. But it did anyway. The (probably illegal) management action backfired. Rather than a few hundred customers catching a glimpse of the T-shirts during the course of the day's work, millions throughout North America saw them through the media coverage of the suspensions; within hours, the union was inundated with phone calls of support and orders for the T-shirts. The truth was out.

Media Hysteria over the Information Highway

By now probably everyone has heard of the information highway, as a result of the massive propaganda blitzkrieg. Announcements heralding the dawn of a new age emanate incessantly and insistently from every quarter. The media gush with the latest info highway reports (but not the fatalities), all levels of government are daily pressured into diverting public monies into yet another private trough, every hi-tech firm, not to mention every hustler and con artist in the business world and academic world, is rushing to cash in on the manufactured hysteria. The aggressive assault on our senses is aimed at securing public support and subsidy for the construction of the new commercial infrastructure. Its message, which has become the mind-numbing multinational mantra, is simple and direct: We have no other choice. Our very survival, it is alleged, as individuals, a nation, a society depend upon this urgent development. Those without it will be left behind in the global competition. And those with it? A "Futurescape" advertisement supplement to the *Globe and Mail* by Rogers Cantel and Bell Canada warned that the information highway "raises the ante in competition. If we don't act, Canada and Canadian companies will be left behind. . . . The information highway is not a luxury technology for the rich. It is the way of the future. And those who do not get on the highway will not have any way of reaching their ultimate destination."

"[Computer] technology is enabling companies to extend their operations and enlarge their profits while reducing their workforce and the pay and security of those who remain."

And what exactly is the destiny advanced by the information highway? Ask the Bell-Atlantic employees. The propaganda never mentions the roadkill, of course, but that is the future for many. Most people in Canada instinctively seem to know this already. According to a 1993 Gallup poll, 41 percent of those currently employed believe they will lose their jobs. But, despite this intuition, people have been terrorized into a hapless fatalism. It's inevitable. Or else they have been seduced by the exciting array of new tools and diversions: home-shopping, home-videos, home-learning, home-entertainment, home-communication. The operative word is home, home is where people without jobs are—if they still have a home. The focus is on leisure, because there will be a lot more of it, in the form of mass unemployment. (Some lucky few will get home-work, as their job takes over their home in the sweatshops of the future.) This is where we are headed on the information highway.

To see where we are headed requires no voodoo forecasting, futuristic speculation, much less federally funded research. We just need to take a look at where we've been, and where we are. The returns are already in on the Information Age, and the information highway promises merely more of the same, at an accelerated pace.

> ***"The [information highway's] focus is on leisure, because there will be a lot more of it, in the form of mass unemployment."***

Technology Replaces and Displaces Workers

In the wake of the information revolution (now four decades old—the terms *cybernetics* and *automation* were coined in 1947), people are now working harder and longer (with compulsory overtime), under worsening working conditions with greater anxiety, stress, and accidents, with less skills, less security, less autonomy, less power (individually and collectively), less benefits, and less pay. Without question the technology has been developed and used to de-skill and discipline the workforce in a global speed-up of unprecedented proportions. And those still working are the lucky ones. For the technology has been designed above all to displace.

Structural (that is, permanent and systemic as opposed to cyclical) unemployment in Canada has increased with each decade of the Information Age. With the increasing deployment of so-called "labor-saving" technology (actually labor-cost saving), official average unemployment has jumped from 4 percent in the 1950s, 5.1 percent in the 1960s, 6.7 percent in the 1970s, and 9.3 percent in the 1980s, to 11 percent so far in the 1990s.

These, of course, are the most conservative estimates (actual unemployment is closer to double these figures). Today we are in the midst of what is called a jobless recovery, symptomatic and symbolic of the new age. Output and profits rise without the jobs which used to go with them. Moreover, one-fifth of those employed are only part-time or temporary employees, with little or no benefits beyond barely subsistence wages, and no security whatever.

In 1993, an economist with the Canadian Manufacturers Association estimated that between 1989 and 1993, 200,000 manufacturing jobs were eliminated through the use of new technology—another conservative estimate. And that was only in manufacturing, and before the latest wave of information highway technology, which will make past developments seem quaint in comparison.

None of this has happened by accident. The technology was developed, typically at public expense, with precisely these ends in mind, by government (notably military), finance, and business elites—to shorten the chain of command and extend communications and control (the military origins of the Internet), to allow for instantaneous monitoring of money markets and fund transfers, and to enable manufacturers to extend the range of their operations in pursuit of cheaper and more compliant labor.

Thus as the ranks of the permanently marginalized and impoverished swell, and the gap between rich and poor widens to nineteenth-century dimensions, it is no mere coincidence that we see a greater concentration of military, political, financial, and corporate power than ever before in our history. In the hands of such self-serving elites—and it is now more than ever in their hands—the information highway, the latest incarnation of the information revolution, will only be used to compound the crime.

Computers Benefit Few

Visions of democratization and popular empowerment via the net are dangerous delusions; whatever the gains, they are overwhelmingly overshadowed and more than nullified by the losses. As the computer screens brighten with promise for the few, the light at the end of the tunnel grows dimmer for the many.

No doubt there has been some barely audible and guarded discussion if not yet debate about the social implications of the information highway, focusing upon such issues as access, commercial vs. public control, and privacy. There is also now a federal advisory commission on the information highway, although it meets in secret without public access or scrutiny, doubtless to protect the proprietary interests of the companies that dominate its membership. But nowhere is there any mention of the truth about the information highway, which is mass unemployment.

For decades we have silently subsidized the development of the very technologies which have been used to destroy our lives and livelihoods, and we are about to do it again, without debate, without any safeguards, without any guarantees. The calamity we now confront, as a consequence, rivals the upheaval of the first Industrial Revolution two centuries ago, with its untold human suffering. We are in for a struggle unlike anything any of us has ever seen before, as the Bell-Atlantic employees testify, and we must use any and all means at our disposal. It's time we came to our collective senses, while there is still time. We must insist that progress without people is not progress. At the very least, as a modest beginning, we pull the public plug on the information highway.

"With the increasing deployment of so-called 'labor-saving' technology . . . , official average unemployment has jumped."

Software as Career Threat

by Philip E. Ross

About the author: *Philip E. Ross is an associate editor at* Forbes *magazine.*

Douglas Flint, 35-year-old owner of Tune-Up Technology in Alexandria, Va., used to make a decent living doing car engine tuneups. Now he gets by. Today's cars don't need tuneups because computerized controls don't wear out. "At the shop level, engine rebuilding is also becoming a dead art," sighs Flint. His mechanics, once well-paid specialists, now survive on general repair work and low-paying routine jobs like oil changes. Many of Flint's competitors have failed.

Computer Software Can Replace the Knowledge Worker

As the auto mechanic has gone, so will go many of today's professionals who make their living by applying specialized knowledge. As computers make the professional's arcana accessible to the layman, potential customers will increasingly handle routine problems themselves, or opt for a software-armed paraprofessional.

To put it more bluntly: Think twice before investing years of your life developing your skills in law, medicine, accounting, travel agentry, financial planning, insurance sales or library science. All these professions are beginning to face serious competition from computer programs. As the software gets better, demand for many professionals, after decades of steady climbing that pushed up incomes, is likely to level off or even fall.

This doesn't mean the end of the knowledge worker. It just means that different kinds of knowledge will be valuable. Machines aren't going to replace surgeons any time soon, but they are gaining on some doctors who earn their living largely through diagnosis. They aren't going to replace merger lawyers, but they can do a lot of damage to lawyers who write simple real estate contracts or do case research.

"There is a lot less knowledge in knowledge work than we realize, and a lot of heavy lifting computers can do," says Paul Saffo of the Institute for the Fu-

From Philip E. Ross, "Software as Career Threat," *Forbes*, May 22, 1995. Reprinted by permission of *Forbes* magazine;

ture, in Menlo Park, Calif. "It will free up people to think, and also cause a lot of pain. It's already happening with lawyers."

Software Can Provide Legal Forms and Research

A lot of legal work consists of pulling up standard contracts and other legal boilerplate from databases. Lawyers (or their paralegals) have been doing this for years and billing clients handsomely for it. Now the clients can do some of that clerical work themselves. Ralph Warner, publisher and cofounder of Nolo Press, in Berkeley, Calif., boasts his company's WillMaker program (about $45 retail) has written more wills than any lawyer alive. Other software packages produce the papers to handle trusts, incorporations and partnerships.

"My guess is that between a third and a half of the work done at big law firms could be routinized," Warner says. "Take maritime law. Every port city has three or four firms that do admiralty work. Now we have the potential for ten lawyers to go to the top of the Rocky Mountains, far from any bit of water, and collect a database to run an on-line system."

In 1994 Cadwalader, Wickersham & Taft, one of New York's oldest law firms, bowed to economic pressures by forcing out 12 partners. Lawyers everywhere learned how expendable they are. Computers have a lot to do with their plight. Junior lawyers—or legal assistants—can, in minutes, do research that used to take hours of page-turning in the library.

"[Many] professions are beginning to face serious competition from computer programs."

"My sense is technology is in the background of tort reform, cost-cutting—all these things eating away at law firms' profitability," says Ethan Katsh of the University of Massachusetts at Amherst, author of *Law in a Digital World.* "Sixty years ago the boundaries of the profession were clearer. You went to law school; it was assumed you knew something others didn't. I'm not sure anyone believes that anymore."

Replacing white-collar clerks has happened before, but never so suddenly. Consider the aspiring bank employee of a century ago: He proved his mettle by doing compound interest and percentage calculations quickly. Now those human skills are rendered worthless by a $13 calculator.

Salesmanship used to be valuable in the distribution of life insurance and mutual funds. It's less valuable now. Fidelity Investments can install a bank of low-paid clerks in Utah to sell financial products via telephone to buyers on Long Island. If their software is good, the clerks can outsell a personable insurance agent who visits customers in their homes.

Like lawyers and insurance salesmen, doctors are threatened by a combination of semiconductors and paraprofessionals. As a category, "physician assistants" date only to 1967, when Duke University graduated the first class. Now the PA profession numbers some 30,000, about half as many as there are doctors in general and family practice. The PAs do pretty much the same work, too, but average just $55,000 to $60,000 a year in income, roughly half of what the average U.S. physician makes.

States have defended their doctors' prerogatives by requiring PAs to work in an M.D.'s office, with rare exceptions for places like rural Alaska. But now that cost-cutting is getting serious and technology is improving, the day will likely come when several PAs can be supervised from a distance by one M.D. Knowledge Industries of Palo Alto, Calif., is working on a head-mounted system enabling ordinary military medics to perform many procedures that now require physicians.

"Lawyers everywhere learned how expendable they are. Computers have a lot to do with their plight."

Hospitals and medical schools already use software to help doctors make their diagnoses or to critique the efforts of students. A program called Iliad, developed by Homer Warner and other doctors at the University of Utah, is in use at dozens of medical schools.

Here's how Iliad works: You enter a patient's age, sex, lab results and symptoms, and the program proceeds through a structured series of queries and answers ending in a range of possible diagnoses. Iliad knows nine subspecialties of internal medicine, encompassing about 1,000 diseases, as well as 1,500 or so intermediate conditions used in the chain of diagnostic deductions. Cost: $995 a copy.

Iliad's publisher, Applied Medical Informatics of Salt Lake City, refuses orders for Iliad from laymen, but it won't be long before good diagnostic software, from this outfit or a competitor, leaks out. When that happens, regular Joes will be able to use the software to get a diagnosis and then call a specialist, reducing the need for general practitioners. Or patients might decide to treat themselves.

Our advice: If you must go to medical school, disregard the usual sermonizing about the need for more family practice physicians, who spend much of their day diagnosing. Instead, consider such specialties as geriatric medicine or general surgery.

But don't go into radiology or pathology. Both disciplines will get a run for their money from software.

David Heckerman, an M.D. and computer scientist, helped design Pathfinder while at Stanford. He says this 30,000-line Pascal program determines if a lymph node is malignant, sometimes more accurately than the expert who provided the knowledge base. "All humans forget things, they get tired," says Heckerman, 38. "The expert system collects an expert's knowledge at his or her best."

The Paradox of Education Requirements

Heckerman, who develops nonmedical products at Microsoft, adds you can put not just doctors and lawyers but also fax machine repairers on a chip, so that their expertise can be provided over a help line at 2 a.m.

Hans Berliner, a computer scientist at Carnegie Mellon, says, with only a little hyperbole: "There is nothing a human mind can do that a computer can't also do, given enough effort."

When a profession loses its grip on its claimed expertise, it tends to respond by raising academic credentials, or getting the government to raise them. The strategy is to restrict entry to the profession while grandfathering the less credentialed people who are already inside it. Schoolteachers spring to mind.

Will this strategy protect doctors, lawyers and other endangered professionals from the computer? The accountants have their hopes. Before the Great Depression, no state required CPAs to have more than a high school diploma. By 1968, 26 states required a bachelor's degree. Now the American Institute of Certified Public Accountants wants the states to mandate 150 semester hours of course work—practically instituting the M.B.A. as a requirement.

Why the rush to add schooling? Barry Melancon, incoming president of the CPA society, cites competition of less credentialed accountants and software packages like TurboTax. "Pure tax compliance is one thing technology will take away from CPAs," he says. "But," he adds, with relief, "unless Congress stops making changes in the tax code, the analysis function of CPAs will continue."

Maybe, maybe not. KPMG Peat Marwick laid off some 230 of its U.S. partners in 1991, the first time it had shed partners for mainly economic reasons. Other Big Six accounting firms followed its example.

Arno Penzias, the Nobel Laureate in physics who is vice president of research at AT&T Bell Laboratories, predicts the market will demand not fancy degrees but experience. "I think we've tied acquiring knowledge too much to school," says Penzias. "What did you do most of the time in school? I daydreamed a lot. It's only on the graduate level, when you're learning by doing, that you stop wasting time."

In his latest book, *Harmony: Business, Technology & Life After Paperwork*, Penzias argues that computerization not only displaces entire departments whose main job is to shuffle paper, but also speeds the rate at which school learning becomes obsolete. "Look, knowledge is not chunks of information, it's a belief about how the world works, a belief we can embody in machinery—like green for go and red for stop," Penzias says. "Knowledge becomes obsolete when the world changes. This will be the first time in history where that happens twice in a single generation."

> ***"Like lawyers and insurance salesmen, doctors are threatened by a combination of semiconductors and paraprofessionals."***

Computer science—the source of all this ferment and angst—offers perhaps the best object lessons in obsolescence. Many universities still offer courses in Cobol, the language used on creaky mainframe systems, even though work in that field is now largely limited to keeping old legacy databases alive. Stay away from these courses. Plenty of former Cobol programmers are now out of work.

Paul Kostek, a systems engineer at Pacific Scientific Software in Seattle, cites another example: those who knit a company's disparate hardware and software into a local area network. "Five years ago no one would have known what a LAN integrator was. Now it's superhot. In a few years, with plug-and-play software and hardware, it'll be dead," he says.

Adaptable professionals will survive. If cataloging is dead, a librarian can make a new career helping library customers troll databases. A computer systems analyst can make his position more secure by developing an expertise in the problems of some industry—such as medicine, retailing or finance—that will remain valuable even if his computer specialty disappears. A travel agent had better find new ways to sell vacation packages, because booking the cheapest flight to Orlando will soon be child's play for anyone with a modem.

The grand illusion of the credentialed professional was that by straining in his youth he could get a ticket to guaranteed income for the rest of a career. Those tickets don't last very long anymore.

Computers Do Not Create Unemployment

by Robert J. Samuelson

About the author: *Robert J. Samuelson is a contributing editor for* Newsweek.

Perhaps within a decade, most Americans will have an e-mail address, just as most now have phone numbers. The computer will become (as it is already becoming) a democratic appliance that will increasingly resemble the kitchen stove. Almost everyone has a stove. But some of us make hamburgers, and others make fettuccini. Computers are the same; they reveal differences more than create them. Once this becomes clear, the idea of cyber inequality will implode.

The Prevailing Theory of Computers and Inequality

Cyber inequality is the notion that computers are helping splinter America economically. They seem one explanation for the sharp increase of wage inequality. Consider this oft-cited comparison: in 1979 a recent male college graduate earned about 30 percent more than his high-school counterpart; by 1993, the gap was 70 percent. The prevailing wisdom among economists is that, as computers have spread, the demand for workers who can use them has increased. Wages for those workers rise, while wages for the unskilled (who can't use them) fall.

What could be simpler: if the problem is no computer skills, then provide skills. Give the poor a tax credit for laptops, suggested Newt Gingrich. Although he retracted that proposal, he didn't disavow the impulse. "[T]here has to be a missionary spirit," he says, "that says to the poorest child in America, 'Internet's for you'." Vice President Al Gore gushes similarly about the Information Superhighway. Technology, if denied, is doom; if supplied, it is salvation.

Inequality Is Due to Business, Not Computers

Bunk. Cyber inequality is mostly a myth. Computers do not really explain widening wage inequalities. The more important cause is a profound change in the business climate, beginning in the 1970s. Economic optimism waned and

From Robert J. Samuelson, "The Myth of Cyber Inequality," *Newsweek*, February 27, 1995; ©1995 Washington Post Writers Group. Reprinted with permission.

competitive pressures intensified. Companies gradually overhauled the ways they pay, promote, hire and fire. Put simply, they began treating their most valuable workers better and their least valuable workers worse.

Everyone knows the pressures that prompted this upheaval: harsh recessions, tougher competition and more corporate debt. Shrinking profit margins reflect the intensity of those pressures. In the 1950s and 1960s, profits before taxes averaged about 16 percent of corporate revenues; they dropped to 11 percent in the 1970s and 9 percent in the 1980s.

When profit margins were fat, companies routinely promoted and provided across-the-board pay increases. The idea was to offset inflation and give something extra. Many companies adopted elaborate "job evaluation" systems that graded jobs across different departments in an attempt to ensure "fairness." Jobs with similar responsibilities would be paid similarly. "The focus was on internal equity," says Paul Platten, a compensation expert with the Hay Group. Companies hired optimistically, because they expected higher profits from higher sales. Young and less skilled workers (the last hired) benefited.

Dropping profit margins devastated these practices. Across-the-board pay increases diminished: In a survey of 317 big companies, Buck Consultants found that 90 percent paid only merit increases. "Job evaluation" systems have been de-emphasized. More money is funneled into pay arrangements aimed at rewarding good performance. In the Buck survey, 30 percent of companies used lump-sum merit increases and 15 percent used "gainsharing." New workers are hired more reluctantly, because companies fear bloating labor costs; entry-level salaries are suppressed. Now the last hired often suffer.

"Cyber inequality is mostly a myth. Computers do not really explain widening wage inequalities."

Computers are only incidental to this process. This does not mean they haven't changed the nature of work or eliminated some low-skilled jobs. They have. For example, the need for secretaries has dropped as more managers use computers. Between 1983 and 1993, the number of secretaries decreased by 14 percent. But this is an age-old process. New technologies have always destroyed and created jobs.

The issue is not whether some people have better computer skills and are rewarded for them; clearly, that happens. So what? Skill differences have always existed. The real question is whether computers have escalated those differences. By and large, the answer is no. Indeed, computers have spread—both at home and at work—precisely because more powerful microprocessors, memory chips and software have made them easier to use. Fewer generic computer skills are needed. As this happens, computers merely complement people's other skills.

Almost accidentally, economists are now confirming that a broader process is fostering inequality. Men laid off between 1990 and 1992 lost an average 20 percent of pay when they got new jobs, says a Census Bureau study. They didn't become less skilled, but they were thrust into a hard labor market. Two-thirds of the increase of inequality does not reflect growing gaps between more and less educated workers (say college and high-school graduates), reports Gary Burtless of The Brookings Institution. Rather, it reflects bigger gaps among workers with similar educations (say, college graduates). Companies are tougher at all levels. Finally, Peter Gottschalk of Boston College and Robert Moffitt of Brown University find that people's earnings now fluctuate more from year to year than they used to; that's consistent with harsher hiring, firing and pay practices.

Contrary to Gingrich and Gore, the Internet is not the promised land. Sure, our economic and social well-being would improve if some of our worst workers had better skills; but the skills they need most are basic literacy and good work habits. With those, computer competence will come if needed. The infatuation with computers as a cause or cure of social distress is misplaced. Mostly, computers mirror who we are: a people of vast vitality, great ingenuity and manifest imperfections.

Computer Technology Reduces Worker Productivity

by Robert Kuttner

About the author: *Robert Kuttner is a nationally syndicated columnist.*

Something is out of kilter in the new information economy. Everything is more automated, but on balance it doesn't seem to save us much time or raise our living standards.

As Technology Increases, Productivity Decreases

Economists have several theories to explain this paradox, but at bottom I think the problem is pretty simple. A lot of the innovation is more trouble than it's worth. Anyone who has wrestled with a new software program and lost, or who wastes time on the receiving end of voice mail or e-mail, will know what I mean.

The technical concept here is productivity. In manufacturing, it takes ever fewer man-hours to build a car or produce a ton of steel. In services, countless clerical tasks are now done automatically.

Yet, oddly, the measured productivity growth of the economy is feeble—an average of less than 2% per year in the 1990s, compared to nearly 4% per year in the 1950s and '60s.

Some economists blame the shift from manufacturing to services. While goods production becomes ever more efficient thanks to machines, there are limits to productivity gains in service occupations.

For example, a schoolteacher, musician, cabdriver, baby-sitter or salesman has a job that inherently doesn't evolve with technology. As the economist William Baumol famously observed, you don't play the "Minute Waltz" more productively by performing it in 50 seconds.

Some others invoke the last refuge of the economist—the lag. Supposedly, we are on the verge of a new burst of growth; it just hasn't arrived yet.

Still others point to the unequal income distribution. Relatively fewer people have the earnings to buy the fruits of all this productivity, so growth stalls.

Each of these stories has a piece of the truth. But the simpler explanation is this: The new information technology produces almost as many costs to productivity as benefits.

Perhaps I'm just grumpy because I spent much of the Labor Day weekend attempting to comprehend a new computer loaded with new software. But, plainly, the frenetic innovation of the information age has the side effect of wasting a great deal of time.

Learning to Use New Programs Wastes Time

No sooner do you learn how to operate a perfectly satisfactory computer program than the cybergeeks come out with another one. Your previous learning is instantly obsolete. Some economist who measures productivity should calculate how much time and money are wasted in the early obsolescence of adequate "last-generation" computers and software.

Given that it takes human beings time to learn how to do things, the knowledge economy may well be innovating at a rate faster than optimal. At some point, the time spent learning how to use these new tools exceeds the time saved.

In addition, the more advanced the technology, the more that can go wrong. Millions of hours are wasted in downtime, not to mention the time spent comparison shopping and just talking about the stuff. Computer banter has overtaken real estate and sports as the second-favorite chat topic and is closing in on sex.

Then there are innovations like voice mail, which may save time for the businesses that use them, but wastes time for everyone else. How many hours have you lost holding the phone listening to gratuitous recorded information before you got the human you wanted in the first place?

Economists measure the productivity gains of the office that replaces its receptionist but not the aggravation to the general public. (If you want to ban voice mail, press one.)

> ***"Plainly, the frenetic innovation of the information age has the side effect of wasting a great deal of time."***

Note that this critique is not Luddite. The problem is not technology, but some of its uses, and its rate of change. Software companies keep innovating with competitors, not consumers, in mind.

Not that the consumer is stupid. On the contrary, the consumer makes the perfectly rational calculation that the time spent learning how to set every digital clock is not worth the slight benefit of having one more appliance displaying the time.

Chapter 1

I love my computer. I am composing these words on it, and it will efficiently dispatch them to my editor. But I can't help remembering that when I started in this business, I composed my prose on a manual typewriter, the type was set by hand—and somehow the paper sold for just a dime. When you netted everything out, it must have been a pretty productive operation. As for quality and output, nobody has matched Shakespeare, and he used a quill.

It requires constant vigilance to keep technology from becoming master rather than servant. So the next time someone suggests an innovation that will waste more time than it saves, just say no. It might improve your productivity.

Chapter 2

How Will Computer Technology Affect the Right to Privacy?

Chapter Preface

Increasingly, business, consumer, and banking transactions are conducted electronically through the use of sophisticated computers. To facilitate this computerized commerce, entire financial histories are kept on electronic file and made available to banks and credit agencies. However, as computer hackers have demonstrated, computerized information can be obtained by anyone with the requisite computer knowledge. Although most people like the convenience and speed of electronic transactions that computers have made possible, many find it dismaying that personal financial information is so easily available to those who might misuse it.

Computer privacy advocates worry that the banks and credit agencies that legitimately collect computerized financial records may wittingly or unwittingly provide private information to intrusive marketers. Though marketers regularly use disparate sources to compile information on consumers, privacy advocates object to the fact that marketers can now use financial databases to ascertain people's income and spending habits and flood these unsuspecting consumers with unwanted solicitations. According to Stanton McCandlish of the Electronic Frontier Foundation, which studies civil liberties issues relating to computer networks, "Every time you use your credit card, . . . corporations can find out everything about you."

But other computer experts contend that fears of computer-aided invasions of privacy are overblown, arguing that computers can as easily enhance privacy as compromise it. Gary Chapman, director of the Twenty-First Century Project at the University of Texas, Austin, notes, "Digital technologies are providing many new ways for people to become anonymous"—including digital encryption, anonymous e-mail networks, and content blocking programs. Software companies already produce programs to block Website ads, Chapman points out, and others produce programs to block pornography that can be adapted to block ads. Further, he maintains, according to already existing laws, individuals must be notified when their financial information is disclosed to someone, and people can simply request that their names be removed from marketers' mailing lists. Therefore, Chapman and others conclude, computers do not pose a serious threat to privacy.

Concerns about privacy on computer networks and the security of databases cover a broad range of topics, from crime to unsolicited sales pitches. The viewpoints in the following chapter present alternative opinions on the effect of computer technology on the right to privacy.

Computer Technology Violates People's Right to Privacy

by David Wagner

About the author: *David Wagner is a writer for* Insight on the News, *a weekly newsmagazine.*

As more than 700 former Republican White House staffers have discovered, the Privacy Act no longer means much in today's highly partisan atmosphere. Given that this atmosphere not only is partisan but computerized as well, it may take laws far more sophisticated to protect the privacy of those about whom the federal government collects information. And that is a very disturbing aspect of the Filegate scandals haunting the Clinton administration. [In June 1996 it was revealed that Clinton White House security staff members had obtained the confidential FBI files of former Reagan and Bush White House staff members.]

Questions About Privacy in the Computer Age

The fact is, technological developments in collecting personal information on Americans are fast outstripping the legal system's ability to account for them. Granted, law traditionally has developed in response to real-world circumstances. Commercial law was preceded by commerce; tort law was preceded by people trespassing on each other's land, hitting each other with sticks and defaming the tavernkeeper's beer. With computers, too, the law will catch up.

But it had better hurry. Here are some questions the U.S. legal system will face:

• How are personal-privacy rights to be protected when data collection that formerly would have taken months of a private detective's time now can be accomplished with a few keystrokes?

• What happens to the notion of limited personal jurisdiction—for example, the fact that courts of Kentucky can't force a citizen of Oregon to serve as a defendant in Kentucky unless that Oregonian has had some sort of meaningful contact with Kentucky—in a world in which one can send data to, and receive data from, computers anywhere in the world?

• How can the Internet become a viable marketplace when any information sent over it, including copyrighted works, credit-card numbers and other sensitive material, can be imperceptibly intercepted?

• Should encryption technology that could solve many of these problems be banned because of the possibility that it could end up in the hands of terrorists and gangsters? And does it matter that the terrorists and the gangsters are going to get it anyway?

Controversy over Encryption Technology

"Encryption" is a fancy word meaning translating information into code to keep it safe from snoops. Encryption technology is software that can restrict data access to those who have a special software "key." The "strength" of encryption technology is measured in "bit-lengths." Encryption technology with a bit-length of 40 or higher is considered "strong." Solveig Bernstein, telecommunications-policy analyst at the Cato Institute, says this threshold is too low. "Netscape uses 40 bit-length encryption," she says, "and hackers break it all the time."

The United States forbids the export of strong encryption technology. The rationale: Such technology might be used by terrorists. True, say opponents of the ban, but given the realities of electronic communication the technology will fall into those hands anyway. Streams of 1s and 0s, transmitted electronically, don't know from border guards or customs officials.

A consortium of Japanese companies already has developed a strong encryption system and intends to market it globally. California-based RSA Corp. also is on the cutting edge of encryption. And, legislation is moving forward to relax the export controls.

For commercial marketers the new possibilities for data collection are a bonanza. Mail-order companies are adept at pinpointing the interests of prospective customers, as demonstrated by the distribution of sales materials or catalogues targeted at—or at least within spitting distance of—their specific interests. Sophisticated list brokers break out lists by 130 qualities of name profile. And that's a lot of snooping.

"How are personal-privacy rights to be protected when data collection . . . can be accomplished with a few keystrokes?"

The fact is, every time someone uses a credit card, even in a store, an electronic trace remains. If a customer buys a book with a credit card, the clerk sweeps the card through the verification machine with its little keypad, then sweeps the purchase with its bar codes over the electronic reader. That credit card now can be matched to specific titles. Over time, a detailed portrait of the customer's book-buying habits can be compiled.

The only way to prevent this is to use cash. In that light, the current talk about "E-cash" and the impending extinction of currency may be ominous.

A Permanent Record of Electronic Transactions

It is possible to create anonymous cash-cards, says Cato's Bernstein, which would have a specific value imprinted on them electronically, and users could spend them down without revealing personal identity. However, the cash-cards would require encryption far stronger than 40 bit-lengths: "Otherwise," says Bernstein, "they can be fiddled so that they never run out. A few of these were made for the Olympics, with $20 on them. They were taken off the market, but they could be out there somewhere. If you have one, you can rig them so that you can buy an unlimited amount of stuff with them—as long as no individual purchase is for more than $20."

Furthermore, every time someone visits a World Wide Web site on-line, he or she leaves an electronic fingerprint. Web sites sometimes brag about how many "hits" they've had or they may tell a user that he or she is the 51,924th hit since last Monday. What people may not know, says Bernstein, is that it is relatively easy for Web-site operators to recover not only the total number of hits but also the source of each. To visit a Web site is to sign its guest book and announce the visit to the world.

Cyber-privacy expert David Post of the Georgetown University Law Center wrote in *The American Lawyer*, a leading professional weekly, that every electronic move people make "can be converted into permanent records that, when combined with innumerable other such records, can form a detailed profile of who we are—the persons and organizations to whom we send messages, the discussion groups in which we participate, the sites on the Internet that we have visited (and the amount of time we spent at each), the goods we have ordered (and those we looked at and chose not to order), and the like."

> ***"Every electronic move people make 'can be converted into permanent records that . . . can form a detailed profile of who we are.'"***

The instant global reach of computerized communications will raise interesting problems of jurisdiction in the courts. In the late seventies, the Supreme Court handled a case in which a plaintiff who purchased a car in New York wanted to sue the distributor when the car exploded in Oklahoma. The suit was brought in Oklahoma. The court held that the Oklahoma state courts could not assert jurisdiction over the New York defendant because even though a car is inherently mobile, a car distributor in New York ordinarily does not foresee being sued in Oklahoma. That's the precedent.

Now suppose a North Carolinian sends E-mail to a friend in Wisconsin. This message libels Mr. X, who lives in California. The E-mail is not adequately encrypted, so it gets out over the Net and ends up in several computers in California, where Mr. X finds out about it. He wants to sue the North Carolinian, but he doesn't want a transcontinental commute to the courthouse, so he sues in California. But the North Carolinian is not in California, has no property there, does not conduct business there and did not intentionally send the offending E-mail there. Is he subject to the jurisdiction of the California courts in this case? Probably not. But the courts may decide to rethink jurisdictional limitations, given that E-mail messages are far more mobile than cars.

Possible Government Uses of Database Information

For many people, the commercial use of data about them represents the computer era's most disturbing threat to privacy. Some social critics argue that in a society in which citizens increasingly define themselves by consumer choices, they inevitably feel naked when they realize that unknown marketing mavens are compiling profiles of them based upon their purchases.

Others say that human beings are more than just their consumer choices, and that computer technology's real threat to privacy comes from its use by government.

Enter Filegate.

It is very easy to put data into a computerized database—and very difficult to get it out. Hitting "delete" doesn't do it: Deleting a file only gets rid of the electronic "pointer" that puts the file on the screen. A pro easily can recover deleted files from a hard drive. Furthermore, even a true deletion won't delete a file from the other computers to which it may have traveled over the Internet.

These facts help explain why the story that the White House secretly has been constructing a massive database on legislators, reporters and contributors has raised eyebrows: This revelation came at a time when the same White House has been caught rifling in FBI files.

"By itself, the database doesn't worry me," says Roger Pilon, a legal scholar at Cato. "It may be just a glorified Rolodex. But if information that was not meant for political databases gets into one—that's another story."

Pilon knows whereof he speaks: He and his wife, Juliana, endured a kafkaesque run of accusations, investigations and hostile leaks at the hands of the Justice Department, for which Pilon worked at the time. The problem stemmed from a misinterpretation of a telephone conversation by his wife that turned up in her FBI background check when she was up for an appointment in the Reagan administration.

"For many people, the commercial use of data about them represents the computer era's most disturbing threat to privacy."

After being exonerated several times over, the Pilons settled a lawsuit against the Justice Department for $250,000. In the wake of Filegate, the executive branch has good reason to reflect upon its future legal liability to other plaintiffs whose FBI files fell into the wrong hands—all the more so because, if anything from those files was put into the White House Office Data Base, it may be too late to erase it or to limit its spread over the Net.

The law may never be able to fully protect Americans from privacy violations through computer technology. But then, tort law never guaranteed that people wouldn't become victims of negligence; contract law never guaranteed that people would always get the benefit of their bargains; and property law never guaranteed that people would receive marketable title to Blackacre. All the law can do is help.

Computer Technology Can Reveal People's Personal Information

by Glen Roberts, interviewed by Vicki Quade

About the author: *Glen Roberts is the publisher of* Full Disclosure*, a periodic newsletter on privacy and technology issues. He is also the host of a weekly radio call-in show, "Full Disclosure Live." Vicki Quade is the editor of* Human Rights*, a quarterly magazine focusing on civil rights issues.*

Vicki Quade: What are the hot issues for your public?

Glen Roberts: Cordless phone privacy comes up a lot, and I tell people, get a police scanner and listen to your own cordless phone calls. See how far away you can pick them up. That's going to open your eyes.

Technology vs. Privacy

When you think that just because your cordless phone doesn't work past the middle of your front yard, that nobody outside your yard is listening, take a police scanner. When you get three blocks away and you can hear your call, that's going to add a different perspective to it.

A lot of people say, yeah, of course you can do that if you have the right equipment. They don't realize that the right equipment is something you buy at a garage sale for $10 or brand new at Radio Shack for $100. They protect themselves by presuming that there's something special or unique about the technology.

I focus on getting people to understand the technology out there, and how, as a society, we try to apply a development.

Is technology creating a second-class status for those who don't have the ability to access all of this information?

That's absolutely true, that we're getting to be the haves and the have-nots, but we're not talking about money, we're talking about information. Or access to information.

It doesn't do us any good if we have a huge library in our house but we don't know how to find what we want. There's a tremendous amount of information available in cyberspace, and if you know how to get it, you can benefit. If you don't understand cyberspace, you're at a loss.

I moved to Oil City, Pennsylvania, from the Chicago area in 1995. John D. Rockefeller started some of his operations here. Quaker State Corporation moved its corporate headquarters from Oil City to Dallas.

There used to be a lot of steel, and active oil wells. The country's earliest oil well is 10 miles away. It was a very rich, very affluent, very industrialized place, but over the past 20 years, it's gone downhill because all of the big companies, all of the oil and all of the steel have gone somewhere else.

And that's why I moved here, because the real estate prices are low. In my business, where I do everything by mail, being able to buy a house for $8,500 makes a big difference.

The Have-Nots Do Not Understand the Technology

The only negative thing is that there was no local Internet available, so it was all long distance calling, which gets expensive.

Right around the time I moved here, the chamber of commerce and various governmental bodies were exploring how to bring the Internet here.

They talked and talked, and I couldn't wait.

What happened is a couple of people, one of them a high school student, just sat down and did it. And they're online.

The city's not online, but we are. Full Internet access. I use a SLIP (Serial Line Internet Protocol) connection, and it's as good.

Meanwhile, the people in this area are spending thousands of dollars researching how to bring the Internet here. They don't understand the whole concept of it yet because they haven't been exposed to it.

I heard about this community development program, where if a corporation invested up to $250,000 in the area, the state would give a matching grant to the city.

So I talked with the mayor of Oil City and said I can put something on the Internet about it and maybe there are some people with corporations in Pennsylvania that would be interested.

> ***"We're getting to be the haves and the have-nots, but we're not talking about money, we're talking about information."***

On Sunday morning, I put a posting up on the Internet. On Monday I was reading my E-mail to the mayor. There was a response from somebody.

The mayor said, "I'm surprised you got a response so soon." Because he doesn't understand that when I put a posting on the Internet, it's not like sending out a mailing, it's not like putting an ad in a monthly newspaper. It's instantaneous. Somebody in Japan, five minutes after I posted that, might well have read that message.

What the Internet can do for an area like this is tremendous because it gives a lot of people exposure to the rest of the world. On the Internet, you're as good as in New York City.

Establishing Standards

What kind of ethical and legal standards do you think are needed in cyberspace?

That's a tough question. Some of it is a matter of control because it's not like the conventional organizations that we have. There are no shareholders, there's no board of directors, no president, no pyramid that you'd have in a normal organization.

Some people might call it anarchy or an information free-for-all. We're starting to see some of the answers with programs like SurfWatch and Netmanning, where you can set standards and limit access to material on your own computer, whether it's because you don't want to see that stuff or you don't want your kids to see it.

When we talk about people using the Internet for criminal activity as opposed to controversial information, I tell people to consider what's done now to catch criminals who do business by phone.

"What we have is a lot of surveillance being done that isn't authorized by a court."

Law enforcement agencies have figured out through wiretaps and other means how to investigate and handle those criminal activities. At no point have we seen law enforcement agencies say drug dealers are doing business by phone, so let's prosecute the board of directors of AT&T for participating in drug dealing.

And yet we see proposals that say we should hold the Internet providers liable for the information there.

What that means is that the providers will run scared and try to stop information that isn't criminal in nature, just because they don't want any problems.

In time, as law enforcement becomes familiar with the technology, we'll see new ways of investigating criminals online, which won't have anything to do with prosecuting the third party that's simply providing the service equally to everyone.

We have to go after the perpetrators, not after somebody providing a service.

You're interested in monitoring government surveillance equipment. What is the latest supersecret stuff?

If you want to electronically surveil, you're supposed to get a warrant. Very few warrants are issued every year. Under 2,000.

Meanwhile, there is a tremendous body of surveillance equipment being sold.

One example is cellular phone monitoring. You can use a police scanner to listen to cellular phone calls, but if I want to listen to your phone calls, good luck. I have to go through 800 channels until I happen to recognize your voice.

With one of these automatic devices, all I have to do is key in your phone number. Any time you place or receive a call, I'm going to hear it. I have to be within the geographic range of the radio waves, that's all.

Of course, to use such a device legally you have to go to a court, and you have to get the same warrant that you would to tap a phone. But across the United States at all levels of government, there are about 1,500 warrants issued a year for wiretapping. Only a few of those are for cellular phones.

Meanwhile, there are a lot of those devices being sold.

Some of them sell in the $20,000 to $30,000 range. But some, like a device made in Canada, can get hooked up to your computer and scanner for about $500.

What we have is a lot of surveillance being done that isn't authorized by a court.

Who Is Looking for What Information?

How safe is the material we're sending, either by fax or over the Internet?

There are two broad categories of people out there looking for information. People just having fun, who listen to cordless phone calls in the neighborhood because it's more exciting than the soap operas. Or they search on the Internet through people's E-mail just because it's fun.

It's certainly an invasion of privacy, but there's no outstanding danger to it.

Then you have another group of people who are actively looking for some piece of information—they want something of value for nothing or they want personal information about you, either because it's a corporate competition or it's someone stalking you.

If someone really has targeted you, there are a lot of ways they can tap into your different communications, from doing a tap on your phone or fax machine to getting a job with the information provider that you have your Internet account with, so that they can view your E-mail.

> ***"If someone really has targeted you, there are a lot of ways they can tap into your different communications."***

About all you can do is to encrypt your information.

But that's become an issue itself, with the government wanting access to encryption codes. You've been touting an encryption program called Pretty Good Privacy.

It's pretty much a shareware program, so you can download it off of the Internet or CompuServe.

Who would want the information most people have online?

If we're putting credit card numbers out, people want it.

Let's say you signed up with a dating service and you met somebody who turned out to be a stalker. That person can sit outside your house with a police scanner and listen to your phone calls. And now they know a whole lot more about you than you would tell them or than they should know.

So when we put information out, it might not seem to be a big deal, but think about all of your phone calls.

Computers Make It Easy to Steal

Unfortunately, there are a lot of people out there looking to commit some type of fraud. If you walk into a bank with a gun, you're probably going to get caught. What if you break into the bank's computer? It's a lot easier to steal.

Now look at software. How many people will copy a diskette of a commercial program for a friend? Will most of those same people go into a store and shoplift something? Once it becomes intangible, people play by different rules.

It doesn't seem like stealing when you copy a disk, so once you've crossed that line, the idea that you can commit a crime silently and anonymously can be appealing.

That makes encryption more important.

Believe it or not, there's more security in writing a letter and mailing it the old-fashioned way. Very few people have access to that envelope. Of those people who have access, very few are going to be inclined to open it, read it, and try to put it back together.

So the mail is safer than the Internet?

I would say so. On the Internet people can search for strings of numbers that look like credit card numbers. Or they could look for particular words or particular names or combinations.

Or medical information?

There's a black market for work histories. Not long ago, about 20 people were arrested for basically stealing personal information and selling it, and quite a few of them were private investigators. Some of them worked for the Social Security Administration, some for local police departments.

If you're an insurance company, or a corporation, and someone either files a workers' comp claim or applies for a job, you might want more information about that person's work history. And who has that information?

> ***"The idea that you can commit a crime silently and anonymously can be appealing."***

The companies that person worked for?

Yes, but you don't know which companies somebody worked at unless they tell you, and if they don't tell you straight, then you don't have that.

So how do you find out?

The Social Security Administration. Every company reports wages paid.

If you call them and ask, How much did Joe Blow make, they won't tell you. But if you hire a private investigator who pays somebody there $50 to run a report for you, that information is free flowing.

You can often find somebody in a company who will give out information for a fee—even if it's one person in 3,000. All you need is one.

So as information gets computerized and more easily accessible, the more we have to worry about how that information will be used.

How Can People Protect Their Privacy?

So what needs to be done to protect that?

That's a tough question. There has to be more awareness of the vulnerabilities of a system, and less free access to all the information.

It really means having less centralized collection of information. Do we need a big database out there?

If I have a particular disease and it's between me and my doctor, it's going to stay there in all likelihood. But if it's between me and my doctor and an insurance company database, then the potential for you and the rest of the world to find out is greatly increased.

"As information gets computerized and more easily accessible, the more we have to worry about how that information will be used."

What's the answer?

We need to operate our lives in a way so our dependence is more on ourselves than on these monolithic institutions that want to collect information.

So you're saying, don't give out information?

Unless it's necessary, don't give it out.

You know, very few people ever check to make sure the information that's already out there is correct. What happens if someone inputs the wrong dates, or facts, or figures? Now the database has that information about you, and it's wrong.

We've lost control of our own information. The way to get it back is to keep it as private as possible.

You get marketing surveys all the time in the mail. How much money do you make, how many kids do you have, how much is your house worth?

The people asking the questions aren't doing it just for fun, they're trying to make some money off of it. Your answers are going into a database, and it's going to be sold.

Is there any way to correct the information out there, or retrieve it so it isn't used?

The only information you have any control over is in regards to your credit history. There are laws that regulate your right to look at your credit history and dispute items there.

When you ask to look at a company's databases, most won't open their records for you.

You have to be careful even about the information you give to the Census Bureau. They assure you that this information is confidential. And they're telling the truth, to a point. What they do is take your census block and report that everyone in that block has an average income of $56,000, a house value of $250,000, and so on.

"We've lost control of our own information. The way to get it back is to keep it as private as possible."

What's the value of that information?

You can buy a program on a CD/ROM, where you type in a zip code and you get the demographics of that area, how much the houses are valued at, what the average income is. A lot of that comes from the census material.

You type in the zip code for Oil City, where I live. If you're a company looking for some big money people, you see that the average income here is $20,000 . . . you say, forget it.

Say you're the IRS and you look at someone's income in Oil City and you see that they're making $500,000 a year. What are they doing? Selling drugs? So you investigate a little about that person.

Or you put in the zip code of Lindenhurst, Illinois, where I used to live. You tell the IRS you're making $3,000 a year. And the databases say the average in that community is $80,000. That raises some red flags that you might be underreporting.

See what I'm getting at. Simple information can be used in a lot of different ways.

So where do you see the whole cyberspace phenomenon going?

We're becoming more dependent on intangible, anonymous, monolithic databases.

We're moving into a world where, in a sense, nothing is real. It doesn't matter who we are or what we are, it matters what information we can present.

And either we're going to be caught up in it or we can use it to our advantage, and a lot of that is learning it and trying to use the technologies that are beneficial for good purposes, as opposed to just sitting back and letting the technology steamroll us over.

Computer Technology Will Eliminate Privacy

by David Brin, interviewed by Sheldon Teitelbaum

About the author: *David Brin is the author of many science fiction novels as well as the nonfiction book* The Blinding Fog: Privacy and Paranoia in the Information Age. *Sheldon Teitelbaum is a journalist and a senior writer for the* Jerusalem Report, *a weekly newsmagazine covering Israel and the Middle East.*

Teitelbaum: In your introduction to The Blinding Fog, *you project two disparate visions. One foresees police cameras on every lamppost. In the other, average citizens can access universal tools of surveillance. Is this our choice—Big Brother or a world of Peeping Toms?*

Brin: Make no mistake, the cameras are coming. Already a dozen British cities aim police TV down scores of city blocks. Crime goes down, but how long before those zoom lenses track faces, read credit card numbers, or eavesdrop on private conversations? You can't stop this Orwellian nightmare by passing laws. As Robert Heinlein said, the only thing privacy laws accomplish is to make the bugs smaller. In a decade, you'll never know the cameras are there. Those with access to them will have devastating advantages.

Equality Through Lack of Privacy

The only alternative is to give the birdlike power of sight to everybody. Make the inevitable cameras accessible so anyone can check traffic at First and Main, look for a lost kid, or supervise Officer McGillicudy walking his beat. Only this way will the powerful have just as much—or little—privacy as the rest of us.

Members of the cypherpunk movement have been promoting encryption as a safeguard of personal privacy. But you don't buy it.

Foremost among reasons why encryption won't work is that secrecy has always favored the mighty. The rich will have resources to get around whatever pathetic barriers you or I erect, while privacy laws and codes will protect those at the top against us. The answer isn't more fog but more light: transparency. The kind that goes both ways.

From "Privacy Is History—Get over It, an interview with David Brin," interviewed by Sheldon Teitelbaum, *Wired*, February 1996.

You think privacy will become extinct?

Like the dodo. But there is a way to limit the damage. If any citizen can read the billionaire's tax return or the politician's bank statement, if no thug—or policeman—can ever be sure his actions are unobserved, if no government agency or corporate boardroom is safe from whistle-blowers, we'll have something precious to help make up for lost privacy: freedom.

Computers Enforce Accountability

You wrote Earth *in 1988 before the Web became a media catch phrase. As a science fiction writer, where did you get it right? And wrong?*

I thought *Earth* would get attention for the ecological speculations and such. Surprisingly, my depictions of a future infoweb raised the most interest. My WorldNet seemed to me a natural outgrowth of what people do with new technology. Some waste time. Others try to elevate the human condition. But most use it as simply another tool, a necessity of life. A routine miracle, like refrigerators and telephones. What intrigues me is how society's contrary interest groups might use infotech—first to mobilize, but then to argue, expose lies, and hold each other accountable. Mutually enforced accountability is the key to running a complex society that can no longer afford big mistakes.

What do you mean by mutual accountability?

In all history, humans found just one remedy against error—criticism. But criticism is painful. We hate receiving it, though we don't mind dishing it out. It's human nature. We've learned a hard lesson—no leader is ever wise enough to make decisions without scrutiny, commentary, and feedback. It so happens those are the very commodities the WorldNet will provide, in torrents. Try to picture multitudes of citizens, each with access to worldwide databases and the ability to make sophisticated models, each bent on disproving fallacies or exposing perceived mistakes. It's a formula for chaos or for innovative, exciting democracy—if people are mature enough.

There's been buzz comparing your 1985 novel, The Postman, *to statements from the militia movement.*

One of a writer's greatest satisfactions comes from inventing interesting villains. But the American mythos always preached suspicion of authority, a basically healthy social instinct that helped keep us free. But the message turns cancerous when it turns into solipsism—the notion that an individual's self-righteous roar has more value than being a member of a civilized society. Solipsism is a rising passion as we near the millennium. In countless popular books and films, the individual protagonist can do no wrong, but every institution is depicted as inherently corrupt. Yet, despite this pervasive propaganda, many resist the sweet lure of self-centeredness. Instead of rage, they offer argument, passion, criticism, even cooperation. *The Postman* was about choosing between solipsism and rebuilding a living community. We all choose each day, in less dramatic ways.

Computer Crimes Will Increasingly Invade People's Privacy

by Gene Stephens

About the author: *Gene Stephens is a professor of criminal justice at the University of South Carolina in Columbia.*

Billions of dollars in losses have already been discovered. Billions more have gone undetected. Trillions will be stolen, most without detection, by the emerging master criminal of the twenty-first century—the cyberspace offender.

Crime in the Future

Worst of all, *anyone* who is computer literate can become a cybercrook. He or she is everyman, everywoman, or even everychild. The crime itself will often be *virtual* in nature—sometimes recorded, more often not—occurring only in cyberspace, with the only record being fleeting electronic impulses.

But before discussing the info highway crimes we can expect to see in the years ahead, let's look at the good news: The most-dreaded types of offenses—crimes such as murder, rape, assault, robbery, burglary, and vehicle theft—will be brought under control in the years ahead by a combination of technology and proactive community policing. Creation of the cashless society, for example, will eliminate most of the rewards for robbers and muggers, while computer-controlled smart houses and cars will thwart burglars and auto thieves. Implanted bodily function monitors and chemical drips (such as "sober-up" drugs and synthesized hormones) will keep most of the sexually and physically violent offenders under control.

More importantly, proactive policies—seeking out crime-breeding situations and taking steps to eliminate them before the crime occurs—may alleviate much of the burgeoning violence among young people. Tender, loving care demonstrated by informed parenting, universal health and day care, mentoring,

From Gene Stephens, "Crime in Cyberspace." This article originally appeared in the September/October 1995 issue of the *Futurist*. Reproduced with permission from the World Future Society, 7910 Woodmont Ave., Suite 450, Bethesda, MD 20814.

and communal attention to children's welfare can prevent another generation of starved-for-attention juveniles from becoming criminals.

Computers Make Crimes Easier

But cyberspace offenders—ranging in age from preteen to senior citizen—will have ample opportunities to violate citizens' rights for fun and profit, and stopping them will require much more effort. Currently, we have only primitive knowledge about these lawbreakers: Typically, they are seen only as nuisances or even admired as innovators or computer whizzes. But increasingly, the benign "hacker" is being replaced by the menacing "cracker"—an individual or member of a group intent on using cyberspace for illegal profit or terrorism.

Access to cyberspace has begun to expand geometrically, and technology is making the information superhighway even more friendly and affordable for millions of users. But foolproof protective systems can probably never be developed, although some high-tech entrepreneurs are certainly trying. Even if a totally secure system could ever be developed, it would likely disrupt the free flow of information—an unacceptable intrusion to most users. In fact, it is the ease of access that is driving this rapidly expanding field of crime.

What are the major cybercrimes being committed, how, and by whom? More importantly, where is cybercrime headed in the twenty-first century? Let's look at six cyberspace crime categories: communications, government, business, stalking, terrorism, and virtual.

Communications Crimes

Already, cellular theft and phone fraud have become major crimes. Low-tech thieves in airports and bus terminals use binoculars to steal calling-card access numbers as unsuspecting callers punch in their phone codes. Other thieves park vans beside busy interstate highways and use equipment obtained from shopping mall electronics stores to steal cellular phone access codes from the air. Within moments of these thefts, international calls are being made with the stolen numbers in what is becoming a multi-billion-dollar-a-year criminal industry.

Phone company employees, meanwhile, are also stealing and selling calling card numbers, resulting in more hundreds of millions of dollars in unauthorized calls. In 1994, an MCI engineer was charged with selling 60,000 calling card numbers for $3 to $5 each, resulting in more than $50 million in illegal long-distance charges. In another case, when a phone company tried to institute a call-forwarding program, crackers quickly defrauded the system of more money than the company stood to make in legal profits.

> **"Anyone *who is computer literate can become a cybercrook."***

In the future, the opportunities for hacking and cracking will escalate, with telephones, computers, faxes, and televisions interconnected to provide instantaneous audiovisual communication and transmission of materials among individuals. The wide appeal of new multimedia communication systems will likely create such a huge volume of subscribers that the price will plummet and make access by all possible. But if billions of dollars of losses to thieves are compounded by billions more required to repair damages created by system terrorists, the cost might become prohibitive to all but the wealthy.

Cybercrimes Against the Government

In 1995, the U.S. Internal Revenue Service instituted stringent new regulations on electronic tax filing and returns. This move was to stop a rash of fraud that cost taxpayers millions in 1994: Returns that were processed quickly via this method turned out to be for tens of thousands of fictitious corporations and individuals. Similarly, in an attempt to stop food-stamp fraud, the government issued electronic debit cards to a trial population and plans to go nationwide with the system later in the decade. However, early reports show that many recipients are selling their benefits for cash—50 cents to 60 cents on the dollar—to merchants who then receive full payment.

Cyberpunks regularly break into government computer systems, usually out of curiosity and for the thrill of the challenge. They often intercept classified data and sometimes even interrupt and change systems. One U.S. Justice Department official reported that military computers are the most vulnerable, "even less secure than university computers." This official noted that, during Operation Desert Storm, hackers were able to track both actual and planned troop movements.

James V. Christy II, director of an Air Force unit of computer-crime investigators, set up a team of hackers to test the security of military computer systems. He reported that the hackers broke into Pentagon systems "within 15 seconds" and went on to break into over 200 Air Force systems with no one reporting or even recognizing the break-ins.

"Increasingly, the benign 'hacker' is being replaced by the menacing 'cracker.'"

Ironically, computer hackers often beat the system using the very technology intended to stop them. For example, federal law-enforcement agencies use an Escrowed Encryption Standard to protect classified information and a chip-specific key to decrypt the system. Experienced hackers can easily discover the key and use it to obtain passwords, gaining full access to encrypted systems.

Newer, more secure encryption systems for protecting government and international business transactions require storing the "keys" in "escrow" with a specific government agency—usually the U.S. Treasury Department. Hackers and civil libertarians find this security solution unacceptable because it impedes the free flow of information and puts almost all sensitive and important data in the hands of government officials. This is seen by many as being dangerous to individual freedoms and a major step in the direction of creating a class structure based on the "information rich" and "information poor."

As more government data is stored in computers, protection will become both more vital and more difficult. When the livelihood of an individual depends on data in government computers, the temptation to "adjust" that record to increase benefits and reduce charges will be great. Many will try to do the adjusting themselves; others will be willing customers for a burgeoning black market of professional crackers. For those who have little need for government benefits but would like to eliminate their tax liability, a highly destructive method would be to plant a computer virus in government computers to destroy large numbers of records. In this way, suspicion would not fall on an individual.

"In the future, the opportunities for hacking and cracking will escalate, with telephones, computers, faxes, and televisions interconnected."

Targeting Business

Today, most banking is done by electronic impulse, surpassing checks and cash by a wide margin. In the near future, nearly all business transactions will be electronic. Thus, access to business computers equals access to money.

Recently, computer hacker John Lee, a founder of the infamous "Masters of Deception" hacker group, discussed his 10-year career, which began when he was 12 years old and included a one-year prison term in his late teens. Without admitting to any wrongdoing, Lee said that he could "commit a crime with five keystrokes" on the computer. He could: (1) change credit records and bank balances; (2) get free limousines, airplane flights, hotel rooms, and meals "without anyone being billed"; (3) change utility and rent rates; (4) distribute computer software programs free to all on the Internet; and (5) easily obtain insider trading information. Though prison was "no fun," Lee admitted that he would certainly be tempted to do it all again.

In a groundbreaking study published in *Criminal Justice Review* in the spring of 1994, Jerome E. Jackson of the California State University at Fresno reported the results of a study of a new group of criminals he called "fraud masters." These professional thieves obtain credit cards via fake applications, or by electronic theft, and pass them around among their peers internationally for profit. These young men and women want the "good life" after growing up in poverty. They are proud of their skills of deception and arrogant enough to feel they won't be caught. Indeed, none of those in the five-year case study were caught.

As seen in the $50-million-plus losses in the MCI case, a far greater threat to businesses than hackers are disgruntled and financially struggling employees. As internal theft from retail stores has always been many times greater in volume than theft from shoplifters, robbers, and burglars, theft by employees armed with inside information and computer access is and will continue to be a much larger problem than intrusion by hackers, crackers, and terrorists combined. By the turn of the century, 80% of Americans will process information as a major part of their employment, according to a United Way study.

In addition, the future portends new and brighter "for-profit" invasion of business computers. As one Justice Department official warns, "This technology in the hands of children today is technology that adults don't understand." The first generation of computer-literate citizens will reach adulthood shortly after the turn of the century and will surely open a new age in the annals of crime and crime-fighting.

Cyberstalking

One frightening type of cybercriminal emerging rapidly is the cyberstalker. Possibly the most disturbing of these criminals is the pedophile who surfs computer bulletin boards, filled with bright young boys and girls, in search of victims. He develops a cyberspace relationship and then seeks to meet the child in person to pursue his sexual intentions. Already recognized as a serious problem, cyberstalking has spawned the cybercop—a police officer assigned to computer bulletin boards in search of these pedophiles. Once a suspect is spotted, the cybercop plays the role of a naive youngster and makes himself or herself available for a meeting with the suspect in hopes of gaining evidence for an arrest.

Also surfing the network, in search of pedophiles, are computer pornography sellers who offer magazine-quality color photographs of young boys and girls in a variety of sexually suggestive or actual sexual acts. Such a ring was broken up in 1994 and was found to have clients in several countries, with the pictures themselves transmitted from Denmark.

Another type of stalker expected to be seen more in the future is the emotionally disturbed loner, seeking attention and companionship through cyberspace, and who often becomes obsessed with a bulletin board "friend." If this person obtains personal information about the cyberspace acquaintance, he or she sometimes seeks a close, often smothering relationship. If spurned, the stalker launches a campaign of cyberspace harassment, moving into real-space harassment if adequate information is obtained. Cyberspace vengeance can take many forms, from ruining credit records and charging multiple purchases to the victim to creating criminal records and sending letters to employers informing them of the "shady background" of the victim.

> ***"As more government data is stored in computers, protection will become both more vital and more difficult."***

In the twenty-first century, with access to the information superhighway available to all and information from data banks networked into dossiers reserved for "official use only" (but easily accessible to hackers and crackers), stalking will not only increase but be facilitated by a new generation of portable computers. Organic nanocomputers may one day be implanted in the human brain, making possible a new crime: mindstalking. Unauthorized intrusion and seduction will reach directly into the victim's brain, making the stalker harder to evade and even more difficult to escape.

Remote Terrorism

In London a couple of years ago, terrorists placed deadly missiles in the back of a truck and remotely sent them flying toward the home of the British prime minister. The missiles exploded on the lawn without harm to the prime minister or the house, but they could have killed him and created an international crisis—clearly the intent of the bombers.

Today, terrorists have the capacity to detonate explosives in another country by means of computers and radio signals bounced off satellites. Because the emerging information superhighway is without borders, computer viruses and other information-destroying instruments can be hurled at business or government officials and facilities from anywhere on the globe.

In the future, information will be so crucial to success in business and personal life that being cut off from it will be like being held hostage or kidnapped. Terrorists who can cut communications off to an individual, group, community, or wider society will have the power and ability to spread fear and panic.

> ***"The future portends new and brighter 'for-profit' invasion of business computers."***

As with stalkers, terrorists will find new opportunities when computer implants in human brains become widely available. Borrowing a twentieth-century technique from psychology—subliminal conditioning—terrorists might recruit unsuspecting accomplices via low-intensity audiovisual messages aimed directly at individuals with brain-implanted computers. Unsuspecting implantees might unconsciously begin to modify their attitudes in the direction sought by the terrorists, or worse, even begin to join in terrorist activities. Political terrorists, whose agenda often is to change the world to suit their beliefs, are the most likely candidates to embrace this new approach and other emerging technologies to gain direct access to the minds of the populace.

Virtual Crimes

Stock and bond fraud is already appearing in cyberspace—stocks and bonds that appear on the markets are actively traded for a short time, and then disappear. The stocks and bonds are nonexistent; only the electronic impulses are real.

In a recent case, a trader was paid $9 million in commissions for what appeared to be some $100 million in sales of bonds. But investigators now feel that these bonds may never have changed hands at all, except in cyberspace. In the future, a virtual-reality expert could create a hologram in the form of a respected stockbroker or real estate broker, then advise clients in cyberspace to buy certain stocks, bonds, or real estate. Unsuspecting victims acting on the advice might later find that they had enlarged the coffers of the virtual-reality expert, while buying worthless or nonexistent properties.

> ***"With access to the information superhighway available to all, . . . stalking will not only increase but be facilitated by a new generation of portable computers."***

This is just the tip of the iceberg in what might be tagged as "virtual crime"—offenses based on a reality that only exists in cyberspace. As virtual reality becomes increasingly sophisticated, it is the young adults in the first decade of the twenty-first century who—having grown up with virtual reality—will create the software and determine the legal and criminal uses of this technology. And with virtual reality potentially reaching directly into the brains of recipients via "organic" computers, the ability to separate cyberspace reality from truth outside cyberspace will be one of the greatest challenges of the twenty-first century.

Twenty-First Century Expectations

The outlook for curtailing cyberspace crime by technology or conventional law-enforcement methods is bleak. Most agencies do not have the personnel or the skills to cope with such offenses, and to date all high-tech approaches have been met by almost immediate turnabouts by hackers or crackers.

As individuals see and talk to each other over computers in the next few years, and as nanotechnology makes computers even more portable, new technology will emerge to protect data. But simplifying systems to make them more universally acceptable and accessible will also make them more vulnerable to intruders.

Control of access by optical patterns, DNA identification, voice spectrographs, encryption, and other methods may slow down hackers, but no method is foolproof or presents much of a challenge to today's most-talented cyberpunks. The trouble is that in the future many more users will have skills far beyond those of today's crackers—a process one expert termed "the democratization of computer crime."

Still, there is much to be gained by easy access to the information superhighway. The "cyberpunk imperatives," a code subscribed to by many hackers, include: (1) information should be free so that the most capable can make the most of it; (2) the world will be better off if entrepreneurs can obtain any data necessary to provide needed or desired new products and services; and (3) decentralization of information protects us all from "Big Brother."

Cybercrime probably cannot be controlled by conventional methods. Technology is on the side of the cyberspace offender and motivation is high—it's fun, exciting, challenging, and profitable. The only real help is one that has not proven very successful in recent decades: conscience and personal values, the belief that theft, deception, and invasion of privacy are simply unacceptable.

Behavioral psychologists argue that all values are learned by a system of rewards and, to a lesser extent, punishment. Thus, if these values are necessary for survival, children should consciously be conditioned to live by them. If all citizens—all computer users—were taught these values and sought to live by them, cyberspace could become the wondrous and friendly place its creators have envisioned.

The Hacker Ethic

Ironically, the greatest possible allies to be found in this search for values in cyberspace are the adolescent hackers of the 1980s, many of whom are the software programmers of the 1990s. In his book, *Secrets of a Super-Hacker*, a hacker named "Knightmare" says that "true hackers" love to break into systems and leave proof of their skills, but do not hurt individuals by stealing tangible goods or money, or destroying files or systems.

"Hacker ethics," Knightmare writes, include informing computer managers about problems with their security and offering to teach and share knowledge about computer security when asked. Increasingly, government and business computer managers are asking. Many of the Fortune 500 companies and numerous government agencies have hired hackers to test their systems and even design new security protocols for them.

"Terrorists who can cut communications off to an individual, group, community, or wider society will have the power and ability to spread fear and panic."

Thus, hackers are helping to protect the information superhighway from crackers and terrorists. As one hacker says, "Hackers love computers and they want the Net safe."

Strong Encryption Is Needed to Protect Privacy

by Whitfield Diffie

About the author: *Whitfield Diffie is an engineer at Sun Microsystems in Chelmsford, Massachusetts, and the inventor of encryption systems for the Internet.*

Like the oceans of 200 years ago, the Internet is a far from safe place. Pirates lie in wait to penetrate computer systems, steal trade secrets and cheat people out of their wares. The only way to secure Internet commerce is by building security into the programs through encryption, the process of scrambling information so that only people who hold the secret keys can decode it.

The Government Wants to Control Encryption

Unfortunately, the strong encryption systems that should be in every spreadsheet, word processor and e-mail program are not readily available. The reason is simple. The Federal Government has refused to allow companies to export such systems, insisting that cryptography is a military weapon. Since the companies can't export these programs, it's not worthwhile to produce them for the domestic market only.

In August 1995, Clinton Administration officials said they were willing to be more flexible about the export of encryption systems. But, unfortunately, their notion of flexibility does not adequately address the concerns of the computer companies.

If the Administration does not fundamentally alter its position, it is likely that our high-tech industries, which sell more than half their products outside the country, will continue to be forced to sell programs with weak security systems that meet export standards or programs that lack security systems altogether. This will pave the way for foreign companies, under fewer constraints by their governments, to grab what is expected to become a huge market for properly safeguarded computer communications.

The announcement is just a reworking of a plan the Government announced two years before. Then, it said that it would allow the export of a strong encryp-

From Whitfield Diffie, "Washington's Computer Insecurity," *New York Times*, August 19, 1995.

tion system which used a mechanism known as "key escrow." The hitch was that this system, called the "Clipper chip," allowed the Government to read all communications encoded with that chip. The Government's principal justification for this scheme was that cryptography could interfere with police wiretapping. The Government played down the more important issue that strong encryption might interfere with our ability to spy on enemies and allies alike.

In addition to its blatant Big Brother aspect, the Clipper chip used secret military technology (an encryption algorithm designed by the National Security Agency) and required that it be embedded in tamper-resistant hardware.

Business leaders and civil libertarians were adamantly opposed to this plan. Not only did the Clipper chip system violate the privacy of individuals, but it was unnecessarily expensive because of the hardware required. Despite this outcry, "key escrow" was adopted as a Federal standard. It bombed in the marketplace.

The new plan the Government hinted at would be a bit of an improvement. It would be carried out entirely in software, and outside escrow agents, rather than Government officials, would hold the decoding keys. These could be obtained with a search warrant.

But "Clipper chip II," as it is dubbed, won't work either. While other nations may share our interest in reading encrypted messages for law enforcement purposes, they are unlikely to embrace a system that leaves them vulnerable to U.S. spying. They will reject any system that gives decoding ability to agents in the United States.

Encryption Must Become More Secure

Our Government also wants to limit the length of keys, and hence the sophistication of the encryption codes it allows for export. Up till now, the Government generally did not allow export of codes with more than 40-bit keys, though in August 1995 it indicated a willingness to increase keys to 64 bits. But during the same week a French computer hacker broke a code with a 40-bit key. Even 64-bit keys are not expected to be adequate.

As for the Government's concern that encryption will interfere with police wiretapping, so far there is little evidence that criminals are hiding their activities through encryption. Furthermore, if such a problem develops, there will be chance enough to rein in cryptography later.

"The only way to secure Internet commerce is by building security into the programs through encryption."

The more pressing problem is the lack of adequate security on the Internet that is stifling business and easing computer penetration by criminals. If Washington will ease its controls on commercial encryption products, industry will be free to build the security mechanisms needed to protect the new medium of world commerce.

Computer Technology Will Not Necessarily Jeopardize Privacy

by Thomas E. Weber

About the author: *Thomas E. Weber is a staff reporter at the* Wall Street Journal.

Anyone who has ventured onto the World Wide Web knows the nightmare scenario.

It's an Orwellian world of privacy invasion and subliminal behavior control. It's a world in which computers log your every move on the Internet, distilling your behavior into individual dossiers that diabolical marketers then use to tailor their pitches to you, the unwitting consumer.

Is the Nightmare Scenario Likely?

So, should you be scared?

It's too soon to tell whether the nightmare scenario will become a reality—online marketers are only now beginning to put controversial tracking tools to work. And few would argue vigilance isn't needed. But there are reasons to believe that the future may not be quite as frightening as some suggest.

For one thing, millions of consumers already divulge information about themselves through price scanners, automated-teller machines, credit cards and all the other means of electronic commerce considered essential. In addition, Internet tracking could actually be convenient for consumers, filtering out all the ads they don't want to see. And for those people who object to *any* tracking, software wizards are working to give them the ability to block Web intrusions.

In fact, even some privacy activists acknowledge that the fears may have been exaggerated. "A lot of self-correcting takes place on the Net," says Jerry Berman, executive director of the Center for Democracy and Technology, a privacy-advocacy group in Washington D.C.

There's no question that the Web has the ability to be extremely nosy.

From Thomas E. Weber, "Browsers Beware: The Web Is Watching," *Wall Street Journal*, June 27, 1996.

For instance, Web marketers can determine, without permission, your "domain," the portion of your e-mail address that follows the @ symbol. That can tell marketers you reached their site via a consumer service such as America Online or a corporate connection. Internet marketers can thus target specific domains for their ads.

> ***"Even some privacy activists acknowledge that the fears [of computer-aided invasions of privacy] may have been exaggerated."***

More controversial are the whimsically dubbed cookies, a technology that allows Web sites to track individual users. For a long time, Web sites could tally requests for information made each day, but they couldn't tell whether one visitor made 100 requests or 100 users made one request each.

With cookies, which have come into use only in 1996, a Web site places a tiny file on a visitor's computer that serves as a kind of tracking beacon. The site doesn't know your name or e-mail address, but it does know that you represent a distinct user. (Curious? Search your hard drive for a file called "cookies" and open it in a word-processing program to see who has served you a cookie.)

Cookies feed some of the more dire privacy scenarios. With them, a Web magazine can see which articles you read; a merchant can tell not only which products you bought, but also which product descriptions you simply *viewed.* (Imagine a supermarket scanner that monitors everything you *look at* in a store.) Similarly, it not only knows which ads work; it also knows which don't.

"If we know you visit a travel site every day, and the next time you come in, we can attach information to your record about what kind of company you work at—that's very powerful," says Kurt Kandler, chief executive of Paradigm, an Atlanta consulting firm with an interactive marketing division. "If we can infer that you might be a frequent flier, that opens up a whole new audience to us."

And that's precisely what chills privacy-minded Web watchers. "When I go into a bookstore, they don't know what books I'm looking at, or what other stores I was just in," says James Howard, a software entrepreneur in Chapel Hill, N.C. "Why do Web sites think they need to know that? Maybe I don't want the cashier knowing that I was browsing the erotic-arts section."

No Name

Still, some of these fears are no doubt overblown. To begin, surfing is an anonymous activity, and cookies can't automatically penetrate that shield. When you visit a Web site, the computer maintaining that site may know your domain, but it can't know your identity, or even your e-mail address, unless you volunteer it. Of course, plenty of sites that sell products on-line require names, addresses, e-mail addresses and credit-card information. Providing it, however, is your choice.

What's more, having your purchases tracked is hardly revolutionary. Many consumers may not realize it, but marketers have been collecting such data on them for years, by analyzing mail-order purchases, magazine subscriptions and supermarket scanner records. The result: Direct-mail solicitations tailored to your interests and checkout-line coupons offered up based on your past shopping habits.

Marketers argue that they are simply taking that personalized targeting a step further. When a visitor returns to a Web site, they say, past behavior can be used to display customized content, or to show ads tied to the interests a user's activities suggest.

"We want to be able to communicate with people on an individual basis," says Taki Okamoto, new-media director at Leo Burnett, an advertising agency in Chicago. "But that just means we want to reach people who are interested in what we're offering."

G.M. O'Connell, partner at high-tech ad agency Modem Media Advertising L.P., Westport, Conn., thinks smarter ads will actually be less intrusive. He is pitching to clients a system of ad "sequencing" whereby specific ads would no longer be shown to users who consistently ignore them. "Three strikes and you're out," Mr. O'Connell says. "We'll figure you're not interested."

Industry observers also point out that targeted ads can command high prices that can help Web-site operators avoid charging users for access. Don Peppers, a marketing consultant and co-author of a book about interactive marketing, says: "If I deliver you [television executive] Barry Diller for 30 seconds, that's a lot more valuable than my shoeshine guy for 30 seconds."

> ***"The computer maintaining [a Web] site may know your domain, but it can't know your identity . . . unless you volunteer it."***

Many people, of course, will be convinced by none of this. For them, the best hope may be the fledgling efforts to fight technology with technology.

Blocking Ads

One of those efforts has been started by Mr. Howard of Chapel Hill. He and some friends have formed PrivNet, a company dedicated to developing privacy-enhancement software. Its Internet Fast Forward product lets users block Web-site ads from popping up on their PC screens. The next version will prevent a Web site from finding out which site a user arrived from. And Mr. Howard says he has ideas on how to make cookies crumble, too.

Other countermoves are in the works. In June 1996, Rep. Edward J. Markey, a Massachusetts Democrat, introduced a bill in Congress that would force companies to disclose what kind of information they collect on visitors to their Web sites and require that users have a chance to remove themselves from marketers' lists. Others have suggested applying PICS (Platform for Internet Content Selection)—a system under development to let users block online pornography—to screen out commercial busybodies.

Meantime, the potential for bad publicity may deter some marketers from pursuing intrusive Web strategies. Julie Kurtzman, coordinator of apparel maker Guess! Inc.'s Web site, says she would relish the chance to plug her site elsewhere based on the viewing habits of visitors to those other sites. But for now, she says, she is too skittish about the privacy issue. She recently received a pitch for software to help track users' activities. "I threw it away," she says.

Chapter 3

Should Computer Content Be Censored?

Censorship of Computer Content: An Overview

by Edwin Diamond and Stephen Bates

About the authors: *Edwin Diamond is a journalist and the director of the News Study Group at New York University. Stephen Bates is a lawyer and a senior fellow at the Annenberg Washington Program in Communications Policy Studies, a nonpartisan think tank. They are coauthors of* The Spot: The Rise of Political Advertising on Television.

Cyberenthusiasts sing the praises of the body electric, a global realm of freewheeling computer networks where speech is open and no restrictive rules apply. But because the Internet ("the Net") exists within societies that have long-standing traditions and laws, its rapid assimilation into the "real world" is provoking tensions and confrontations that are now being played out in the legal domain.

Legislating Speech Restrictions on the Internet

In spring 1995, for example, the U.S. Senate passed the Communications Decency Act, authored by Sen. James Exon (D-Nebr.), a bill that would give the Federal Communications Commission the power to regulate "indecency" on the Internet. A number of state legislatures are considering similar legislation. Net enthusiasts and systems operators argue that the Exon bill and proposals like it are unconstitutional as well as unworkable: if a literary magazine put its contents online, for example, and included a short story with a four-letter word, the law could leave the editor liable for a $50,000 fine and six months in jail. Speaker Newt Gingrich, professed cyberspace enthusiast, also opposes Exon; the bill [was signed into law in February 1996, but was struck down by a federal appeals court in June 1996. It will be reviewed by the Supreme Court in 1997]. Following the Oklahoma City explosion, Sen. Dianne Feinstein (D-Calif.) introduced a bill to crack down on bomb-making guides on the Internet, an understandable, if somewhat emotional, reaction to domestic terror acts. The Feinstein bill [was dropped from the final version of the Antiterrorism and Ef-

From Edwin Diamond and Stephen Bates, "Law and Order Comes to Cyberspace," *Technology Review*, October 1995.

fective Death Penalty Act of 1996]. Meanwhile, several states are considering bills to criminalize "online stalking"—repeatedly making cybercontact with an unwilling subject. Connecticut has enacted one into law.

Whatever the fate of these regulations, in the legislatures and in the courts, the concerns they reflect won't go away. Battles over the boundaries of online free speech have erupted with increasing frequency as the Internet has grown in population and in public awareness. The Net is a breeding ground for all kinds of expression, some of it lyrical and wise, but some of it vile and hateful, all of it easily accessible to anyone who logs on. Because freedom of expression is generally contested only when the speech is repugnant, the cases that have arisen tend to focus on the seamier side of the Net.

"Because freedom of expression is generally contested only when the speech is repugnant, the cases that have arisen tend to focus on the seamier side of the Net."

Indeed, a major factor driving such legislation is the prevalence of pornography in cyberspace. A Carnegie Mellon study found 68 commercial "adult" computer bulletin board systems (BBSs) located in 32 states with a repertory of, in the researchers' dry words, "450,620 pornographic images, animations, and text files which had been downloaded by consumers 6,432,297 times." Concerned by these findings and attempting to comply with Pennsylvania's obscenity laws, the university banished many Internet "newsgroups" that offered sexually explicit photographic images, movie clips, sounds, stories, and discussions, noting that Pittsburgh-area high schools had access to these newsgroups through the Carnegie Mellon system. Under fire for censorship, the university restored the text-only sex newsgroups, but not the ones carrying photographic images.

Five Difficult First Amendment Issues

The Net has thus become a First Amendment battleground. The resolution of the ensuing legal battles—some of which are likely to reach the Supreme Court—will help shape the conduct and culture of computer communications in the decades ahead. These conflicts revolve around a few fundamental questions.

1. How far does the Constitution go in protecting repugnant or defamatory speech on the Net?

In 1995, University of Michigan undergraduate Jake Baker was arrested by FBI agents for posting to the alt.sex.stories newsgroup a violent narrative of rape and torture that used the real name of a female classmate for the victim. Baker subsequently e-mailed a friend that "just thinking about it [his fantasies] doesn't do the trick anymore. I need to do it." The university suspended him and a federal judge ordered him held without bail, charged with the federal crime of "transporting threatening material" across state lines.

Some civil liberties groups rushed to the student's defense, arguing that the Constitution guarantees freedom even for repugnant fantasies broadcast worldwide. In June 1995, a federal judge in Detroit implicitly agreed, throwing out the case. While the university acted properly in disciplining the student for his behavior, the judge ruled, there was no cause for a criminal indictment.

The press critic A.J. Liebling once observed, "Freedom of the press is guaranteed only to those who own one." On the Internet, for better or worse, everybody "owns" a press. Baker did not have to send his grotesque tale to a series of kinky magazines until one finally accepted it for publication; he, like any other Internet user, could simply upload his word-processed file to alt.sex.stories, where no editor checks for spelling or grammar, let alone merit.

The young woman could still bring civil action against Baker for libel. When *Penthouse* published a piece of short fiction about the sexual adventures of a "Miss Wyoming" a few years ago, the real Miss Wyoming sued. Her case was thrown out because the piece was unambiguously fictional, but a Baker-like case, where the writer knows the subject, might reach a jury. . . .

Differing Standards of "Obscenity"

2. Laws and mores differ among towns, states, and countries. Whose rules apply in cyberspace?

Say that a New York City user downloads a favorite Sherlock Holmes story from a London computer. The works of Arthur Conan Doyle are in the public domain in the United Kingdom but some are still under copyright in the United States. Which country's law prevails? Or what happens if a member of the California bar offers to answer legal questions on a Usenet newsgroup. Is the attorney guilty of practicing law without a license outside California? *Penthouse* has created a World Wide Web edition whose first page instructs: "If you are accessing Penthouse Internet from any country or locale where adult material is specifically prohibited by law, go no further." Is that disclaimer enough? Or would *Penthouse* executives be wise to avoid any travel to a puritanical country where they might face prosecution? Such questions will pop up with increasing frequency as the Internet becomes more popular. . . .

One need not even leave the United States to encounter a broad range of standards on acceptable forms of expression. Consider the saga of Robert and Carleen Thomas, a married couple in their late 30s living in California's Silicon Valley. Until 1991, Robert had churned through a series of white-collar sales jobs on the fringes of the valley's booming, high-tech industries. Then he and Carleen found their own entrepreneurial niche. Working out of their tract home in Milpitas, they started the Amateur Action Bulletin Board System (AABBS), which enabled subscribers to download sexually explicit images and

"On the Internet, for better or worse, everybody 'owns' a press."

join in chat groups to discuss the materials.

The Thomases' digitized collection reached 20,000 images, largely gleaned from a photographer friend who once worked for *Playboy* and from magazines published abroad. The most frequently downloaded images depicted partially clad children, bestiality, and bondage. The Thomases promoted their service as "the nastiest place on earth," and advertised on the Net that they accepted Visa and MasterCard. By 1994, AABBS had more than 3,600 subscribers, each paying $99 per year for the privilege of accessing the collection.

Too Nasty for Tennessee

Unhappily for the Thomases, they received too much publicity. In mid-1993, a Tennessee man surfing the Net came across an AABBS publicity post in the form of suggestive picture captions. The surfer, upset by what seemed to him to be child pornography, notified U.S. Postal Service authorities in Memphis. These officials activated Operation Longarm, a government anti-obscenity drive that focuses on child porn and, most recently, computer networks. As Longarm officials see it, the anonymous nature of the Internet makes it the perfect place for pedophiles to lurk.

> ***"One need not even leave the United States to encounter a broad range of standards on acceptable forms of expression."***

The Memphis authorities assigned the complaint to postal investigator David Dirmeyer, who joined AABBS (under the alias "Lance White") and began downloading its images and tapping into its chat groups. Based on Dirmeyer's findings, postal investigators raided the Thomases' home in January 1994, armed with a 32-page search warrant, and seized computers, videotape-dubbing machines, and the AABBS database of photographs and videotapes. The couple was indicted, tried in federal district court in Memphis, and convicted of distributing obscene materials in interstate commerce. In December 1994, Robert Thomas was sentenced to 37 months; Carleen to 30 months.

The Thomas case reveals the difficulty of interpreting, in a world of computer networks, the meaning of "community standards"—the test by which a piece of work is to be judged obscene, according to the legal doctrine that the Supreme Court established in its 1973 decision in *Miller v. California*. In *Miller*, the Supreme Court ruled in effect that residents of Bible Belt towns need not put up with Times Square raunch. But in cyberspace, where physical proximity to an information source is unimportant, *Miller*-style community standards are essentially unenforceable.

Civil libertarians worry that if the Thomases' convictions hold, the Net will be governed by the standards of the most restrictive communities in the nation. In appealing their conviction, the Thomases argue that the materials they offered were not obscene by the standards of their Bay Area community. In fact, in 1992 the San Jose high-tech crime unit—essentially the Thomases' hometown police—seized the AABBS computers, scrutinized the collection of images, and found them insufficiently offensive to justify prosecution. . . .

Access Providers' Responsibility for Content

3. When offensive expression is distributed on a computer network, who is accountable?

Are people who post pornographic pictures to a Usenet newsgroup liable for obscenity in, say, Memphis, given that they had no way of knowing where images might be downloaded? Would they be liable if children downloaded the images? For that matter, would the operators of an Internet access service in Memphis be liable for importing obscene material into town, or for making pornographic material (which adults can legally view) unlawfully accessible to children, merely for providing the conduit over which users reached such postings? The law is still murky on these questions of accountability.

As more and more people gain Net access through their schools and employers, such institutions are facing an uncertain future. At Santa Rosa Junior College in California, two female students were the subjects of sexually derogatory comments on a chat group restricted to male students. The women filed a civil rights claim against the college, arguing that the group violated federal law by excluding women and that the messages—discussing the two women in graphic "bathroom wall" language, according to one description—constituted sexual harassment. The students demanded that the journalism instructor who ran the online system be fired for aiding and abetting the harassment. The school hastily settled the suit, awarding the women cash compensation for both complaints and putting the instructor on indefinite administrative leave—and, in the process, exerting a considerable chilling effect on the people who run online services at other universities.

Academia isn't the only place where online sexual (or sexist) chatter will collide with freedom of speech. For example, if employers provide desktop access to Usenet discussion groups, including the gamy alt.sex hierarchy, could they be sued by women workers for creating a "hostile workplace"? In the past, courts have ruled that tacking up *Playboy*-style centerfolds on office bulletin boards can constitute sexual harassment of female workers—is the display of such images on computer screens any different?

> ***"The Thomas case reveals the difficulty of interpreting, in a world of computer networks, the meaning of 'community standards.'"***

The question of responsibility is also pivotal in a suit that Stratton Oakmont, a brokerage firm based in Lake Success, N.Y., brought against the Prodigy online service. Individuals sent a series of postings accusing Stratton Oakmont of criminal behavior and violations of Securities and Exchange Commission rules to Prodigy's "Money Talk" forum. Stratton Oakmont sued

Prodigy for $200 million in libel damages. Prodigy lawyers argued that the service is a passive carrier of information, like the telephone company. Stratton Oakmont, however, countered that Prodigy is in the publishing business and is therefore responsible for all communication on its service.

"When offensive expression is distributed on a computer network, who is accountable?"

A New York state judge ruled that Prodigy, which routinely screens postings for obscene or potentially libelous content, does in fact exert a form of editorial control over content on its system and could be sued as a publisher. Prodigy is appealing the state court's decision. (The man accused of writing the messages, a former Prodigy employee, says someone forged his ID. Such impersonation is relatively easy for even a journeyman hacker, and is bound to become more common—further muddying the waters of responsibility.)

In deciding whether Prodigy is liable for libelous material posted by its users, the appeals court will have to rely on few—and ambiguous—legal precedents. One court ruled that CompuServe was not responsible for material placed on its system by a subcontractor. Another court, however, held that a bulletin board operator was liable for copyright infringements perpetrated by its users. One certainty: if systems operators are deemed responsible, they will monitor users much more closely—and pass on the cost of new staff to their customers. User fees will increase as Net access providers spend money on legal fees fighting off lawsuits.

Protecting Children

4. How can children be insulated from the Net's raunchier material?

A few years ago, protesters in Fresno, Calif., used a magnifying glass to find offensive textbook illustrations, including what they termed "phallic bicycle seats." A group in suburban New York City claimed that it had spotted a drawing of a topless bather in a beach scene in one of the *Where's Waldo?* children's books. After the threat of legal action, the book was removed from the school library shelves. It doesn't take a magnifying glass to find hard-core pornography on the Internet—and since many youngsters can navigate circles around their elders on the Net, some adults are in a near panic.

Not without reason. In one afternoon of online prospecting, we unearthed instructions for making bombs, an electronic pamphlet called "Suicide Methods," and a guide for growing marijuana at home. Besides NASA photos of Jupiter, worldwide weather reports, and the Library of Congress catalog, kids can access *Penthouse*, *The Anarchist's Cookbook*, and the poisonously anti-Semitic tract *Protocols of the Elders of Zion*. It is as if every modem owner in the world—including porn fans, skinheads, bazooka lovers, anarchists, bigots, harassers, and Holocaust deniers—selects the books for everyone else's school library. As President Bill Clinton told a meeting of the American Society of

Newspaper Editors in spring 1995, "It is folly to think that we should sit idly by when a child who is a computer whiz may be exposed to things on that computer which in some ways are more powerful, more raw, and more inappropriate than those from which we protect them when they walk in a 7-11."

Any user of the Internet can post pornography or sexual invitations to any unmoderated Usenet group: according to the Toronto arts paper *Eye Weekly*, a Canadian recently sent a detailed post on oral sex to newsgroups populated by children. Moreover, the facelessness of the Net makes it impossible to determine who is accessing information. The manager of an adult bookstore can recognize and eject a 12-year-old; the operator of an Internet file archive cannot.

Computer Safeguards vs. Computer Whiz Kids

Several companies are now developing "lock-out" Internet accounts that block access to certain regions of the Net known to contain material inappropriate for children. Many online services, public schools, and universities block out particular Usenet groups—often all of the alt.sex groups; sometimes only the most repugnant, such as alt.sex.pedophilia. Some sites have modified the Internet search tool Veronica to reject requests that include, for example, the word *erotica*. The American Library Association and other anticensorship organizations are keeping a watchful eye on these efforts to guard children—ready to oppose measures that tip the scales too far away from protection of free speech.

In any case, Net-savvy kids can breach such safeguards. If a school's Usenet system blocks the alt.sex groups, for example, a sufficiently motivated young hacker can use a common Internet tool called telnet to gain access to a system that does offer them. Such surfing gets even easier with the online menu system called gopher; the user can start at a "clean" site and, sooner or later, reach a "dirty" one. We started from the U.S. Department of Education's gopher server, for instance, and in seven gopher hops reached "The School Stopper's Textbook," which instructs students on how to blow up toilets, short-circuit electrical wiring, and "break into your school at night and burn it down." On the World Wide Web, with its tens of thousands of hyperlinks, similar short hops can whisk a student from a stuffy government site to an X-rated one. Even without access to gopher, telnet, or the Web, students can find plenty of inappropriate material; automated servers in Japan and elsewhere send out individual postings, including those from the alt.sex hierarchy, to anyone who sends the proper command through e-mail.

> ***"Besides NASA photos of Jupiter . . . and the Library of Congress catalog, kids can access* Penthouse *[and]* The Anarchist's Cookbook.*"***

Most states have laws against giving children pornography, and some also prohibit providing minors with "dangerous information" (for example, guides to building explosives). Thus, in hopes of limiting their liability, many school districts are requiring parents to sign forms before their children can have Internet accounts—in effect, permission slips for virtual field trips. The lawyers drafting the documents are treading a fine line. A form vaguely referring to the possibility of "offensive material" may not hold up in court as proof that consent was adequately informed. On the other hand, a parental form that is too specific, spelling out the multifold possibilities of pornography, racism, sexism, munitions manuals, and all the rest, may frighten mom and dad into keeping the kids offline altogether—or into shopping for another school district.

"The [computer] user can start at a 'clean' site and, sooner or later, reach a 'dirty' one."

Schools will do the best they can to corral children in safe cyberspaces. But will that be enough? Many onliners worry that Congress will in effect mandate that the entire Internet become a child-safe "Happynet." The political pressures may indeed prove irresistible, especially now that the Christian Coalition is lobbying for laws against online pornography. A Happynet Act would violate the First Amendment, but litigating the case up to the Supreme Court could take several years and hundreds of thousands of dollars. . . .

Brave New Networks

These and other situations reflect the growing conflict between the law and computer-network technology. The legal mind constructs a time and computer-network space-bound world; cybernauts inhabit a world where physical location is immaterial. "Our laws didn't envision the Internet," says Larry Kramer, professor of constitutional law at New York University. In a notable effort to bridge the gap, a new Center for Informatics Law has been established at the John Marshall Law School in Chicago. The center promotes the need to create a separate set of principles just for cyberspace that may depart from the old common-law system.

Rhetorically, at least, the conflict between the old spatial laws and the new Net technology has been one-sided. The technologists are better poets, and they have appropriated the most vibrant images to advance their cause. Indeed, the Progress and Freedom Foundation, a conservative Washington think tank, produced a document with the less-than-modest title "Magna Carta for the Knowledge Age." The document talks grandly, if somewhat vaguely, of "liberation in cyberspace" from "rules, regulations, taxes and laws"—calling for, among other things, the abolition of the Federal Communications Commission.

In this way, the eager explorers of cyberspace like to draw a parallel between the emergence of the new world information order and the development of the frontier in the American West. This is the conceit promoted by the Electronic Frontier Foundation, which has been working since 1990 to promote online civil liberties. But we find two metaphorically opposed images of "the frontier."

One is the heroic, colorized frontier of romantic fiction and television and movies, populated by manly sheriffs and spunky womenfolk. The other is the actual frontier, where life was often nasty, brutish, and short.

Eventually, in both fiction and fact, civilization arrived, bringing with it rules, social order, and taxes. To all but die-hard survivalists, this was regarded as progress. The Internet is now undergoing a similar transition, as the new, inchoate medium of unfettered individual freedom begins to evolve. The Wild West of the cyberfrontier is already morphing before our eyes—on the screen and in the courts.

Computer Content Should Be Censored

by Arianna Huffington

About the author: *Arianna Huffington is a senior fellow at the Progress and Freedom Foundation (a nonprofit organization dedicated to creating a positive view of the future), where she chairs the Center for Effective Compassion.*

If there is one problem with the Communications Decency Act signed into law in February 1996, which makes it illegal to post "indecent" material on the Internet, it is its name [the law was struck down by a federal appeals court in June 1996]. Discussions of indecency and pornography conjure up images of *Playboy* and *Hustler*, when in fact the kind of material available on the Internet goes far beyond indecency—and descends into barbarism.

Most parents have never been on the Internet, so they cannot imagine what their children can easily access in cyberspace: child molestation, bestiality, sadomasochism and even specific descriptions of how to get sexual gratification by killing children.

The First Amendment vs. Indecency

Though First Amendment absolutists are loathe to admit it, this debate is not about controlling pornography but about fighting crime.

There are few things more dangerous for a civilization than allowing the deviant and the criminal to become part of the mainstream. Every society has had its red-light districts, but going there involved danger, stigmatization and often legal sanction. Now the red-light districts can invade our homes and our children's minds.

During a March 1996 taping of a "Firing Line" debate on controlling pornography on the Internet, I was stunned by the gulf that separates the two sides. For Ira Glasser, executive director of the American Civil Liberties Union, and his team, it was about freedom and the First Amendment. For our side, headed by Bill Buckley, it was about our children and the kind of culture that surrounds them.

From Arianna Huffington, "Internet Evils Beyond the Decency Limits," *Washington Times*, March 16, 1996. Reprinted by permission of the *Washington Times*.

There are three main arguments on the other side, and we are going to be hearing a lot of them as the ACLU's challenge to the Communications Decency Act comes to court.

Arguments Against Censorship

The first is that there is no justification for abridging First Amendment rights. The reality is that depictions of criminal behavior have little to do with free speech. Moreover, there is no absolute protection of free speech in the Constitution. The First Amendment does not cover slander, false advertising or perjury, nor does it protect obscenity or child pornography. Restricting criminal material on the Internet should be a matter of common sense in any country that values its children more than it values the rights of consumers addicted to what degrades and dehumanizes.

Civilization is about tradeoffs. And I would gladly sacrifice the rights of millions of Americans to have easy Internet access to "Bleed Little Girl Bleed" or "Little Boy Snuffed" for the sake of reducing the likelihood that one more child would be molested or murdered. With more than 80 percent of child molesters admitting they have been regular users of hard-core pornography, it becomes impossible to continue hiding behind the First Amendment and denying the price we are paying.

Parents Cannot Always Protect Children

The second most prevalent argument against regulating pornography on the Internet is that it should be the parents' responsibility. This is an odd argument from the same people who have been campaigning for years against parents' rights to choose the schools their children attend. Now they are attributing to parents qualities normally reserved for God—omniscience, omnipresence and omnipotence. In reality, parents have never felt more powerless to control the cultural influences that shape their children's character and lives.

The third argument that we heard a lot during the "Firing Line" debate is that it would be difficult, nay impossible, to regulate depictions of criminal behavior in cyberspace. We even heard liberals lament the government intrusion such regulations would entail. How curious that we never hear how invasive it is to restrict the rights of businessmen polluting the environment or farmers threatening the existence of the kangaroo rat.

> ***"Most parents have never been on the Internet, so they cannot imagine what their children can easily access in cyberspace."***

Yes, it is difficult to regulate the availability of criminal material on the Internet, but the decline and fall of civilizations throughout history is testimony to the fact that maintaining a civilized society has never been easy. One clear sign of decadence is when abstract rights are given more weight than real lives.

It is not often that I have the opportunity to side with Bill Clinton, who has eloquently defended restrictions on what children may be exposed to on the Internet. When the president is allied with the Family Research Council and Americans for Tax Reform is allied with the ACLU, we know that the divisions transcend liberal vs. conservative. They have to do with our core values and most sacred priorities.

Internet Access Providers Should Censor Content

by Cathleen A. Cleaver

About the author: *Cathleen A. Cleaver is a lawyer and the director of legal studies at the Family Research Council, a conservative national organization devoted to promoting traditional family values.*

Anyone awake during January 1996 has heard that CompuServe has blocked 200 pornographic sites from its subscribers worldwide in response to an imminent German prosecution. Some hysterical commentators and technogeeks warn that this action marks the demise of Freedom itself. Other less vocal people quietly hope that CompuServe will make this temporary solution a permanent one.

How Pornography Is Sold on the Internet

Consistent in the public debate over the German situation is a lack of understanding of the basics of the technology and the laws of our country. Fundamental Internet pornography education is long overdue.

Take CompuServe and Germany. Three facts about the German situation are widely misunderstood. First, the sites were Usenet newsgroups. Second, CompuServe did not eradicate the newsgroups, but simply removed them from its system. Third, the sites contained child pornography and hard-core pornography.

It does not matter which sites CompuServe blocked, because cyberspace is cyberspace, right? Wrong. Different "protocols" are used to access different parts of what is generally termed the "Internet." The Internet is actually a network of networks, not each of which is the same. The distinction between networks is important for legal and practical reasons.

CompuServe "blocked" Usenet newsgroups. Usenet newsgroups are sites which are accessible by subscribers to online services through the providers' local server. In other words, with the Usenet, a service provider acts as a wholesaler or distributor who "stocks" certain newsgroups in its local server, which

From Cathleen A. Cleaver, "Who's Responsible for Controlling Cyberporn?" *Washington Times*, February 1, 1996. Reprinted by permission of the *Washington Times*.

can be thought of as a warehouse. Online service providers choose which groups to put in their warehouse, and subscribers then "order" newsgroups from the warehouse to be "delivered" to their computers. Online service providers play an active role in stocking and delivering Usenet newsgroups to their subscribers.

CompuServe, therefore, did not really "block" the newsgroups, but, rather, removed them from its local server. They still exist in cyberspace, and savvy computer users can get to them, but not with CompuServe's help.

The Usenet Is Not the Web

It is a mistake to equate the Usenet with the World Wide Web, another major Internet "network." Online service providers do not "stock their shelves" with Web sites like they do with newsgroups. The Web is so named because it resembles a weblike interface of avenues of communication. The Web can be thought of as a city with many intersecting streets. Online service providers give their subscribers "browsers," computer programs which can be thought of as cars, which subscribers can use to "get to" locations in the city. Subscribers can drive their cars to good neighborhoods or bad ones, as they choose. Online service providers can build special expressways to certain locations, or advertise for or own certain locations in the city. But generally, they do not play as active a role in Web communication as they do in Usenet communications.

"CompuServe's decision to remove newsgroups containing child pornography and obscenity is more than good business, it is mandated by U.S. law."

CompuServe has no legal obligation to provide any pornography to its subscribers. CompuServe's removal of child-pornography and obscene newsgroups was entirely appropriate and reasonable, notwithstanding hysterical rhetoric to the contrary. Indeed, to the burgeoning "mainstream" Internet market not interested in deviant sexual discussions or images, CompuServe's action was not only tolerable, but laudable.

CompuServe's decision to remove newsgroups containing child pornography and obscenity is more than good business, it is mandated by U.S. law. Critics decry the injustice of Americans' freedom being curtailed because of Germany's laws. Not so fast—many if not most of the newsgroups removed by CompuServe would be found illegal upon prosecution in the United States, too; CompuServe's potential liability is just as real here. Besides, the question could be: why should Americans have the right to force Germans to accept this filth? Far from creating jurisdictional conflict, the German situation shows that two diverse nations concur in their intolerance for child pornography and graphic or deviant pornography. In fact, every developed country with a statutory system that addresses sexual crimes forbids trade in child pornography.

For now, CompuServe has made cyberspace for its subscribers a little bit safer than it was. There is no reason why CompuServe should ever restore newsgroups with child pornography and obscenity. Its reputation as a market leader that cares about responsible corporate citizenship is not undeserved. A decision to permanently discontinue these newsgroups would relieve legal liability concerns in Germany and the United States, and would undoubtedly be rewarded by appreciative new subscribers.

In Support of Decency

Congress has been grappling with the problem of online pornography since 1994. The Communications Decency Act (CDA), drafted by Sen. Jim Exon, Nebraska Democrat, is now part of the 1996 telecommunications law. [The CDA, signed into law in February 1996, was struck down by a federal appeals court in June 1996. It will be reviewed by the Supreme Court in 1997.] The CDA presents the strongest and most effective approach to combating cyberporn which our Constitution will allow. Principally, it closes a gap in the current federal law by prohibiting the computer distribution or display of indecent material to minors.

The "indecency" standard has a long history of surviving court challenges by friends of the porn industry. Further solidifying the constitutionality of this standard, the Supreme Court in January 1996 twice refused to review decisions in *Action for Children's Television vs. FCC* involving challenges to indecency regulations. No, the indecency provision will not find Shakespeare or any other serious work of literature to be indecent. Indecent material is defined as patently offensive depictions of sexual or excretory activities or organs. History shows that common sense has not let honest inquiry confuse art and literature with patently offensive materials which degrade women, corrupt children and ruin men.

If the telecommunications bill should pass, online service providers and users will be charged with ensuring that indecent sexual material within their control is not available to children. That will include the terrible 200 newsgroups removed by CompuServe, and undoubtedly many more. Individual and corporate citizens who cherish children would not expect any lesser duty. "None can love freedom heartily, but good men; the rest love not freedom, but license."

Hate Speech on the Internet Should Be Challenged

by Abraham Cooper

About the author: *Abraham Cooper is a rabbi and associate dean of the Simon Wiesenthal Center in Los Angeles, a Holocaust memorial and study center.*

Nineteen-ninety-six marked a turning point for the growth and impact of the Internet. Clearly, it has established itself as an important gatekeeper of communications and ideas throughout the world.

Growth of the Internet

Consider that there are already 100,000 connected networks—representing an annual growth rate of 85%—ten million host computers, and thirty million users in 186 countries. The World Wide Web, that area of the Internet which provides the greatest opportunity to market and promote ideas and products, already has 76,000 Web servers representing an incredible 2400% rate of growth between 1995 and 1996.

The main reason for this unprecedented phenomenon is clear. For the first time in the history of our civilization, people have been empowered with a technological tool to directly and instantaneously communicate across the street or around the world. Combined with the relatively low cost of the Internet and the general absence of rules and regulations, it can truly be said that the Superhighway of Information is a breakthrough for personal freedom of expression and global democratization. If this is the case, then why is the United Nations Centre for Human Rights so concerned? Why did the recently convened G-7 [group of seven most industrialized nations] meeting with Russia on international terrorism specifically single out the Internet as a source of deep concern? Why are human rights watchdog organizations like the Simon Wiesenthal Center devoting significant portions of their research efforts to monitor the Internet? The basic answer is quite clear: the very same tool which offers unprecedented opportunities to educate and uplift humanity can and is being utilized by a small but committed number of groups seeking to promote agendas ranging from terror-

From Abraham Cooper, "The Challenge of Hate on the Internet," a paper delivered to the United Nations Centre for Human Rights, Geneva, Switzerland, on September 10, 1996. Reprinted by permission of the author.

ism to racial violence and derisiveness. The so-called lunatic fringe has embraced the Internet with a passion and frightening level of sophistication.

Extremist Groups and the Internet: The Missing Link?

You will notice that a good portion of the analysis presented in this viewpoint focuses on developments in North America, particularly in the United States. There are a number of reasons for this approach. First and foremost to date, the Internet has been embraced more profoundly in the United States than in any other country in the world. In fact it is suggested that nearly half of all American adults already have access to this new technology. Secondly, while political extremism, xenophobia, racism and antisemitism have global manifestations, the United States is home to the largest number of identifiable indigenous white supremacist and neo-Nazi hate groups.

As of 1996, as part of its worldwide monitoring of such groups, the Simon Wiesenthal Center monitors some 250 American organizations which promote racism, antisemitism and violence. Experts estimate that there are between 25,000 and 100,000 white supremacists in the United States. In addition, the new phenomenon of the so-called Militia movement, with its radical antigovernment rhetoric, has attracted tens of thousands of other Americans.

In the last decade, leaders of such groups like extreme right-wing politician David Duke have succeeded in gaining national notoriety, financial support and recruits via talk shows, cable and satellite television, short wave radio and self-promoting publications. However, even with this previously unprecedented exposure to the American public, none of these individuals or groups has succeeded in generating a mass movement. Among the crucial missing elements: a sustainable, attractive and affordable marketing plan, one which would enable them to tap into the group most susceptible to their message of hate and terror—young people.

Virtually overnight, all that has changed.

Extremists have embraced the varied forms of communication offered by the Internet. Anonymously posted "spamming" via e-mail enables bigots to launch on-line hate attacks—sometimes to tens of thousands of unsuspecting recipients—with little fear that they will ever be identified, let alone held accountable for their actions. On-line discussion or chat groups provide an opportunity to denigrate minorities, promote xenophobia and identify potential recruits. In addition, law enforcement organizations throughout the world have expressed deep concern that those elements of the Internet strictly designed for confidential communications are being utilized to promote illegal activities. Such tools as encryption (encoding) and IRCs (on-line conferencing) can be used, for example, by terrorists to coordinate deadly activities.

> ***"Extremists have embraced the varied forms of communication offered by the Internet."***

Greatest Source of Hate Postings: The World Wide Web

To date, however, the greatest level of activity by extremists that we have been able to monitor on the Internet is to be found on the World Wide Web. As of August 1996, the Wiesenthal Center has identified over 200 problematic Web pages. Currently they are classified in the following categories:

- Nationalist/Secessionist
- Explosives/Anarchist/Terrorist
- Neo-Nazi/White Supremacist
- Militias
- Holocaust Denial
- Conspiracy

The World Wide Web provides many advantages to the extremist. Prior to the Internet, traditional modes of communication left the hate messenger and his message on the fringes of the mainstream culture. Not anymore. Today, the Internet provides hate-mongers a remarkably inexpensive means to promote their "product" to a potential audience of tens of millions of people worldwide. Secondly, in the past, limited funds meant that most extremists saw their messages relegated to unattractive flyers, pamphlets, or poor quality videos—hardly the type of material guaranteed to attract young people used to CDs and high-tech games. The currently available multimedia technologies (including audio and video) on Web pages ensure that the "quality" of presentation and the "attractiveness" of hate and mayhem rival or surpass any other hi-tech presentation available to audiences. Further, the interactivity of the Internet has led to the emergence of an "on-line subculture," where different sites promote and reinforce agendas of hate, anarchy, and terrorism. For example, a Web page devoted to Hate Music may be promoted by another venue which provides explicit and all-too-accurate data on how to build a car bomb or make napalm. That same location would then encourage the user to "visit" another site which serves as a clearinghouse of information for on-line extremist groups. No one should be surprised, therefore, that there have been a number of tragic incidents—primarily in North America—involving teenagers who have downloaded bomb-making instructions and actually built these instruments of death.

"The interactivity of the Internet has led to the emergence of an 'on-line subculture,' where different sites promote and reinforce agendas of hate, anarchy, and terrorism."

So what can be done to slow down or reverse this troubling trend on the Internet? To date, the Wiesenthal Center has had various levels of contact with authorities in Australia, Canada, Great Britain, Italy, Germany, and of course, the United States. The Wiesenthal Center has also raised this matter with officials at UNESCO [United Nations Educational, Scientific, and Cultural Organization], the OECD [Organization for Economic Cooperation and Development], the OSCE [Organization for Security and Cooperation in Europe] and the European Parliament. In addition, we have had significant contact with Internet Service Providers (ISPs) in the United States and Canada. The results of these contacts have been varied and mixed and in general reflective of the confusion over who, if anyone, is responsible for the posting of information on the Internet.

As a result our main focus has been with the on-line community and service providers in North America. In this regard the prevailing laws of the United States deserve special mention.

Worldwide Hate and the U.S. First Amendment

Many of the extremist groups disseminating their messages of hate, racism and bigotry rely upon the protection offered by the First Amendment of the United States Constitution as justification of their activities. The United States, of course, has a strong tradition of interpreting the freedom of speech in the broadest fashion possible. Hence, it is unlikely that any significant effective legislation in the United States *vis-à-vis* Internet postings will occur except in the areas of bomb-making and on-line criminal or terrorist activities.

(The special significance of this factor is clear. Materials that are treated as illegal in most other democracies outside of the United States, including that which has been deemed dangerous, racist or defamatory under the laws of other societies, will be presented on the Internet via U.S. postings and as a result are accessible to virtually everyone around the globe—regardless of existing local laws and mores.)

As a result of this reality, our main focus in the United States has been with the private sector—in this case, the on-line community. In fact, there is a strong tradition in the United States that the gatekeepers of communications and the media exercise responsibility and restraint when presented with requests by avowed racists and extremists for unencumbered and unfiltered access to the public. Newspaper editors and radio and television station managers do so, not because of any legislation, but based on the understanding and acknowledgement that the unique powers of the media in American society bring with them special responsibilities to the community.

> ***"With the advent of the Internet, . . . the known and accepted limits placed upon our broadcast media no longer apply."***

Thus, despite the protection afforded to racist, hate-inspiring speech, by the First Amendment, it has been possible to marginalize such messages by limiting unfiltered access by broadcast and print media, both publicly funded as well as private sector. As a result, it would be, for example, difficult for the Ku Klux Klan to obtain broadcast time on American television to air a live cross burning.

With the advent of the Internet, however, and particularly the tools available via the World Wide Web, the known and accepted limits placed upon our broadcast media no longer apply. Rather than one hundred radio stations or one-hundred-channel cable television access, we now have the capacity to have literally millions of broadcast outlets, each of which has full access to broadcast media tools once available to a very limited elite.

"There is almost an assumption . . . that somehow American interpretations of freedom of speech laws should be the only guiding principle when it comes to regulating the Internet."

The resulting challenges are daunting to those of us in the United States who are dedicated to maximizing speech and marginalizing the agenda of bigots. For the rest of the world, the abuse of the Internet by those supporting terror, mayhem, racial violence, antisemitism and xenophobia presents an unprecedented challenge to existing anti-racist and anti-hate tradition and law since much of this material emanates from foreign sources, especially and including the United States.

Promoting Acceptable Use of the Internet

To complicate matters, there is almost an assumption among many within the Internet community in the United States that somehow American interpretations of freedom of speech laws should be the only guiding principle when it comes to regulating the Internet. Of course, it is not the U.S. Wide Web, but the World Wide Web. Many meetings will be needed to help other nations to participate in defining the directions of a technology that will shortly embrace much of how information is transmitted around the globe.

Meanwhile, the Simon Wiesenthal Center has attempted to engage the on-line community in the United States and Canada on these issues. We have already made a modest proposal to the more than 1,000 businesses providing Web page hosting services to adopt the acceptable-use policies currently used by all other media outlets in the United States, from newspapers and magazines to billboards and telephone yellow-pages-standards that have been generally successful in marginalizing this type of bigotry.

Frankly, the U.S. Internet community's response has been mixed at best. However, we are convinced that as the scope and depth of the services available via the Internet expand worldwide, policies governing the Internet that both afford citizens around the world with the rights of speech and protections from hate, racism, terror and mayhem can and must be formulated. I can assure you that the Simon Wiesenthal Center is devoting tremendous resources to helping address these complex issues and is committed to work with governments, non-governmental organizations, media and the on-line community to find functional answers to these challenges.

I would like to end on a positive note. The Simon Wiesenthal Center has just completed our first year [1996] on-line ourselves. Our multilingual Website includes an on-line tour of our Museum of Tolerance, biographies of children whose lives were affected by the Holocaust, surveys on important issues like race and ethnicity, as well as a CyberWatch section that allows individuals to report incidents of racism and hate-mongering. So far we have had more than 75,000 visitors from over 80 countries around the globe. In 1997, we plan to digitize our Multimedia Learning Center and to establish a "Cyberclass" online that will allow teenagers around the world to discuss these issues in real-time.

The Internet with all its world-changing potential is here to stay, and it is our hope that with due diligence, this revolutionary new media can bring about the tremendous benefits that its early developers and promoters have envisioned.

Computer Content Should Not Be Censored

by Marc Rotenberg

About the author: *Marc Rotenberg is director of the Electronic Privacy Information Center (EPIC), an organization that supports litigation for computer privacy rights.*

A copy of *The Naked Society* sits in my office. Some people might think it is a collection of dirty pictures. Not at all.

It's a book written by Vance Packard, the author of three national bestsellers, about the growth of surveillance and the loss of personal freedom. Packard used "naked society" to describe how new technology strips us of our privacy. The book begins with a quote from a famous judge and ends with the Bill of Rights.

The Effects of Political Control of Content

Now give some politician the ability to do a global search and delete, and I have little doubt that all electronic copies of books such as *The Naked Society* would be erased overnight from the Internet.

Think I'm exaggerating? Here's what happened when Bavarian prosecutors told CompuServe, Inc., to pull the plug on newsgroups with "sex" in the title. The fan club for Patrick Stewart, the actor who plays Capt. Jean-Luc Picard on *Star Trek: The Next Generation* and does an excellent one-man performance of *A Christmas Carol* at holiday time, got zapped. The reason? The newsgroup is alt.sexy.bald.captains. Also knocked off the 'net by zealous thought police was a support group for disabled people (alt.support.disabled.sexuality) and a parody of an annoying children's television character (alt.sex.bestiality.barney).

Of course, censorship isn't just about sex. The Chinese government recently told Reuters and the Dow Jones News Service that they could no longer provide economic information to the country without government approval. Why? To protect economic security. And the government of Singapore continues its campaign to ensure that speech is sanitized before it reaches the minds or hearts of its citizens.

From Marc Rotenberg, "The 'Net Doesn't Need Thought Police," *Computerworld*, February 19, 1996. Reprinted by permission of the author.

The U.S. is getting drawn into this craziness because religious zealots and their allies in Congress have decided they know what is good for us and our children. Telling others what they should read, think or believe is about as un-American as it gets. But through the Exon-Coats Communications Decency Act, which passed in February 1996 as part of the Telecommunications Deregulation and Reform Bill, such nonsense has become the law [the act was struck down by a federal appeals court in June 1996].

The Internet: A Radio or a Bookstore?

Supporters of this act say it's nothing more than old-fashioned regulation of TV and radio. Anyone who uses the 'net knows that's completely wrong. (Not surprisingly, a sponsor of the Communications Decency Act proudly proclaims he doesn't use the 'net.)

Regulating the Internet isn't like regulating radio or television. No World Wide Web site operator is licensed. No scarce spectrum is used. Regulating speech on the Internet is like telling bookstore owners, newsstand operators and librarians which books to stock and which magazines to sell. It's like the government telling people who use the telephone which words they can use.

Supporters of the legislation say it will protect children from the evils of dirty pictures. That's crazy, too. Young kids aren't interested in dirty pictures. Like all campaigners against sexuality, all the publicity-seeking moralists have accomplished is to splash the stuff they most fear across the front pages of the nation's newspapers. They might as well put a blinking arrow on top of the *Playboy* home page and say "Don't look here!"

> ***"Regulating speech on the Internet is like telling bookstore owners, newsstand operators and librarians which books to stock and which magazines to sell."***

Of course, parents should be free to select materials that are appropriate for their children and Internet users should be able to reject material that is objectionable. If you really don't like an on-line service's policy or content, cancel your membership.

But be careful when people tell you which words you can speak and which books you can read. Once they start drawing lines they rarely stop. Parody, criticism, satire, adult conversation, literature and art all would become suspect.

The legislation gives federal investigators the right to comb through Web sites, newsgroup posts and even private electronic mail to find evidence of indecent speech. Use a word that someone doesn't like and you could get thrown in jail. The bill even threatens the right to use privacy technologies, such as encryption, because the government now will have the right to open private E-mail if it suspects the message contains offensive language. Flaming becomes a criminal offense.

The Importance of the First Amendment

The supporters of government censorship will say they don't intend to eliminate the acceptable stuff, just the bad stuff. And that's exactly the problem the First Amendment was designed to avoid. It gives us the right and the responsibility to decide for ourselves what is objectionable and what isn't. It forces us to make choices when we are confronted with controversial ideas and new viewpoints. We don't need the First Amendment to protect greeting card prose. We need it to protect the openness and diversity of a free society.

The timing for this congressional nonsense couldn't be worse. The U.S. has a vital role to play in the new on-line environment as defender of free speech and open debate. Many countries will be tempted to impose restrictions because of culture, for economic security, for national security or simply to intimidate opponents. Political leaders in the U.S. should stand up against the thought police, not join their ranks.

We all have an interest in opposing censorship. No matter what your views, they may be illegal somewhere. If each country imposes a filter on information there may be little content left.

Vance Packard wrote in *The Naked Society*, "the Bill of Rights represents a magnificent vision for assuring the Blessings of Liberty." Those are important words. Kids should have a chance to read them before the high-tech moralists sweep the books off the shelves of cyberspace.

Internet Access Providers Should Not Censor Content

by John Perry Barlow

About the author: *John Perry Barlow is a cofounder of the Electronic Frontier Foundation, an organization that promotes awareness of and supports litigation on issues of civil liberties and computer networks.*

Two weeks ago, a prosecutor in Munich managed, almost casually, to strike a global blow against freedom of expression. Though he is a person of such obscurity that most of the accounts I've read of this incident didn't even mention his name, he has been able to constrict the information flow for some 4 million people in 140 countries.

He did this merely by telling CompuServe, the world's second largest online-service provider, that it was breaking Bavarian law by giving Germans access to Usenet discussion groups believed to include explicit sexuality. A strangely terrified CompuServe responded by removing any newsgroups whose title contained the word sex, gay or erotic, thus blocking access to all subscribers, not just those in Germany. Given the centralized nature of its operations—and the decentralized nature of Usenet—this was, according to CompuServe, the only way it could comply.

Thus were CompuServe subscribers prevented from further discourse on whatever they talk about in *alt.sex.bestiality.hamster.duct-tape* (which may exceed even my high squeamishness threshold). At the same time, however, they were also barred from *alt.religion.sexuality* (a pretty chaste topic), *clari.news.sex* (which redistributes wire-service stories) and *alt.sex.marsha-clark* (the mind reels . . .).

Once again, the jackboots of the Industrial Era can be heard stomping cluelessly around the Infobahn. In fact, the Germans did almost nothing to stanch the flow of sexual materials. The newsgroups that CompuServe removed are still active on millions of computers worldwide. CompuServe subscribers in Bavaria or anywhere else can simply switch to a less timid online service and

From John Perry Barlow, "Thinking Locally, Acting Globally," *Time*, January 15, 1996.

re-enter the discussion. As Internet pioneer John Gilmore once said, "The Net interprets censorship as damage and routes around it."

Such assaults are most likely to injure the large service providers, sober institutions more culturally attuned to their governmental attackers than the info-guerrillas of cyberspace. CompuServe, for its cowardice in folding without a fight, probably deserves the calumny heaped on it by angry users. The company says it hopes to reopen access to all but its German subscribers as soon as it can figure out how.

"As Internet pioneer John Gilmore once said, 'The Net interprets censorship as damage and routes around it.'"

But the issue at stake here is larger than whether the good people of Munich can prevent others half a world away from looking at pictures of sexually misused hamsters. These apparently trivial struggles may in fact be the opening fissures of a historical discontinuity.

The real issue is control. The Internet is too widespread to be easily dominated by any single government. By creating a seamless global-economic zone, borderless and unregulatable, the Internet calls into question the very idea of a nation-state. No wonder nation-states are rushing to get their levers of control into cyberspace while less than 1% of the world's population is online.

What the Net offers is the promise of a new social space, global and anti-sovereign, within which anybody, anywhere can express to the rest of humanity whatever he or she believes without fear. There is in these new media a foreshadowing of the intellectual and economic liberty that might undo all the authoritarian powers on earth.

That's why Germany, the People's Republic of China and the U.S. are girding to fight the Net, using the popular distaste for prurience as their longest lever. After all, who is willing to defend depictions of sexual intercourse with children and animals? Moving through the U.S. Congress right now is a telecommunications-reform bill that would impose fines of as much as $100,000 for "indecency" in cyberspace. Indecent (as opposed to obscene) material is clearly protected in print by the First Amendment, and a large percentage of the printed material currently available to Americans, whether it be James Joyce's *Ulysses* or much of what's in *Cosmopolitan* magazine, could be called indecent. As would my saying, right here, right now, that this bill is full of shit.

Somehow Americans lost such protections in broadcast media, where coarse language is strictly regulated. The bill would hold expression on the Net to the same standards of purity, using far harsher criminal sanctions—including jail terms—to enforce them. Moreover, it would attempt to impose those standards on every human who communicates electronically, whether in Memphis or Mongolia. Sounds crazy, but it's true.

If the U.S. succeeds in censoring the Net, it will be in a position to achieve far more than smut reduction. Any system of control that can stop us from writing dirty words online is a system that can control our collective conversation in other, more important ways. If the nation-states perfect such methods, they may own enough of the mind of mankind to perpetuate themselves far beyond their usefulness.

If that sounds overstated to you, consider the millions of people one prosecutor in Germany was able to mute with little more than an implied threat.

Hate Speech on the Internet Should Not Be Censored

by Leslie Harris and Jill Lesser

About the authors: *Leslie Harris is the director of public policy and Jill Lesser is the director of the Civic Media Project at the People For the American Way Action Fund.*

Editor's note: This testimony was submitted to the Senate Judiciary Committee's Terrorism, Technology and Government Information Subcommittee during hearings to consider adding prohibition of bomb-making instructions on the Internet to the Antiterrorism and Effective Death Penalty Act of 1996.

People For the American Way Action Fund (the "Action Fund") submits this testimony to emphasize the importance of the First Amendment in discussions concerning government control of speech on the Internet and other online networks. The Action Fund is a 300,000-member organization committed to preserving the central values of the First Amendment by promoting tolerance, free expression and vigorous public debate. We applaud Chairman Arlen Specter and the Judiciary Committee for holding this hearing on these issues of critical importance in the information age.

Violent Speech in American Society

The American political landscape for years has been populated with people who spread reckless and violent rhetoric. Such rhetoric and the debate that it has spurred in the aftermath of the April 1995 bombing of the Murrah Federal Building in Oklahoma City is particularly troubling to the Action Fund, which is committed both to protecting freedom of expression and to promoting a climate of tolerance and community. We believe that when presented with difficult issues like how we should respond to political figures who tell supporters that their opponents are out to destroy American society or to broadcasters who tell their listeners or viewers that the government is the enemy of the people, feeding fears that this nation's family, faith and freedoms are under imminent threat

From the congressional testimony of Leslie Harris and Jill Lesser before the Senate Committee on the Judiciary, Subcommittee on Terrorism, Technology, and Government Information, May 11, 1995.

of destruction, the answer is not to silence such speech but to encourage more speech in response.

We are at the same time very concerned about the existence of "hate speech" and are unwilling simply to join the chorus of people who claim that such speech has absolutely no impact on behavior. We believe very strongly that ideas do indeed have consequences. We do not believe that the existence of such consequences, however, makes the case for government censorship. Instead, we must respond to intolerant and violent rhetoric by encouraging Americans to stand against those voices and emphasize the American values of liberty, justice and respect for the differences inherent in a vibrantly pluralistic society. The "marketplace of ideas" strengthens democracy when everyone takes the responsibility to be engaged in the debate. We advocate not censorship, but citizenship.

"Policy makers should not use [the Oklahoma City bombing] to undermine the positive unifying aspects of speech on computer networks."

In the wake of the horrible bombing in Oklahoma City, citizens of this nation are rightly concerned with activities that appear to threaten the safety of American citizens. But the Action Fund believes that we must not let that incident diminish this nation's commitment to the First Amendment. Policy makers should not use this tragic incident to undermine the positive unifying aspects of speech on computer networks and the value those networks add to society. The Internet and other online computer networks are already transforming the way people in this country and around the world communicate, entertain themselves and behave as political creatures. The fact that these new technologies offer powerful modes of information dissemination cannot alone justify government intervention and intrusion into the constitutional rights of American citizens. If we do so, the value of such networks will diminish, leaving this nation's role in the information age and the values of the First Amendment threatened.

The Government Should Not Censor Speech

The Action Fund acknowledges that the specific intent of this hearing is to address the narrow questions raised by the government's power to investigate and infiltrate the purveyors of violent or mayhem-inducing computer communications. And, we agree with the general conclusion of the testimony being presented at this hearing by Jerry Berman of the Center for Democracy & Technology that the federal government already has ample investigative and surveillance tools to ensure adequate protection of the American public from violent speech on the Internet.

However, we are submitting our own testimony because we also feel strongly that the question of whether the government should control, track or investigate violent speech in the new online environment is only one among many dilemmas that have surfaced in response to the proliferation of computer networks and their apparent ubiquity. For example, just in the first three months of the 104th Congress [January through March 1995], we have seen significant attention paid to legislative proposals that seek to restrict the transmission of sex-related or adult material on the same computer networks.

While the legal analyses may differ slightly in particular circumstances, the Action Fund believes that it is inadequate to address government response to violent speech in the online environment without recognizing that content regulation in one subject area sets precedents for content regulation in other areas. This Committee must scrutinize very carefully any efforts to restrict or monitor any category of speech online which could not lawfully be restricted or investigated in a bookstore, library, newsstand, town square or other context.

The Internet and other computer networks are unique. They enable Americans to become publishers of information with the stroke of a key. In that way such networks operate like distributors of newspapers or pamphlets put out by individual citizens. Resources like the World Wide Web greatly expand the sources of information available to individuals in their own homes and enlarge the impact that any one citizen with relatively few resources can have on public debate.

Free Computer Speech Enhances Democracy

The inherent potency of these networks in shaping debate must not be used to justify government monitoring and censorship. Instead, it should be seen as an opportunity to enhance democracy—to encourage more Americans to use these technologies to respond to rhetoric they find either helpful or abhorrent. While the tragedy in Oklahoma has made many in this country question the implications of unfettered speech in several arenas, most specifically in the media, it is important to remember that speech in this country often serves its highest value when it challenges our beliefs and values. It is a basic tenet of American society that effective discourse emerges most readily out of heated emotions, be they positive or negative. And it is through effective discourse that conflicts are often peaceably solved.

One of the most disturbing elements of the recent attempts to censor speech on the Internet and other computer networks is the general lack of familiarity with the technology and the resulting willingness by policy makers to enact restrictions of speech, rather than explore the ability of the technology itself to empower users to make decisions about the kinds of content to which they have access. The debate during this Congress has largely centered on the Communications Decency Act (S.314), introduced by Senators James Exon and Slade Gorton, and [enacted in February 1996 as part of the] telecommunications reform legislation. [The

"Content regulation in one subject area sets precedents for content regulation in other areas."

Communications Decency Act was struck down in June 1996 by a federal appeals court. It will be reviewed by the Supreme Court in 1997.] That legislation would establish an outright ban on speech that is indecent, lewd, lascivious or filthy but nonetheless fully protected by the Constitution, without any examination of the legislation's First Amendment implications or the technological tools that may be available to enable adult users to make personal content decisions.

> ***"The inherent potency of these networks in shaping debate must not be used to justify government monitoring and censorship."***

The Action Fund urges this Committee to recognize that the Internet and other computer networks hold vast possibilities for the reinvigoration of democratic discourse in this country. Neither the unfamiliarity with the technology nor the fear invoked by recent acts of random violence or the worry about access by our nation's children to adult-oriented materials should lead Congress irreparably to damage the usefulness and importance of those networks without a complete examination of both the constitutional implications of restricting certain speech and all facets of the technology.

Chapter 4

Should Universal Access to Computer Technology Be Guaranteed?

Computer Haves and Have-Nots: An Overview

by Charles S. Clark

About the author: *Charles S. Clark is a staff writer for the* CQ Researcher, *a weekly news and research publication of Congressional Quarterly, Inc.*

An unintended consequence of the information revolution, according to many observers, is the widening gap between the information haves and have-nots. It has been dubbed "the civil rights and economic rights issue of the 21st century," "information apartheid" and "electronic redlining."

Computer Haves and Have-Nots

Currently [as of 1995] only 10 percent of Americans have the know-how and $1,000-plus worth of equipment—computer, modem, telephone connection and gateway software—needed to cruise the information superhighway. A survey by *PC World* concluded that households with incomes of $50,000 and up are five times more likely than others to own a personal computer and 10 times more likely to have access to on-line services. The gap is racial as well as economic. A 1993 Census Bureau study found that 37.5 percent of whites have computers at home, work or school compared with only 25 percent of blacks and 22 percent of Hispanics.

Only 20 percent of public libraries are hooked to the Internet, according to the American Library Association (ALA), the vast majority of them in urban areas. Only 12 percent of the classrooms in U.S. schools have a telephone jack, but only 4 percent of all classrooms are wired to the Internet, according to the National Education Association.

This is why a coalition of groups that includes the NAACP, the Consumer Federation of America, the Center for Media Education, the National Council of La Raza and the United Church of Christ in 1994 petitioned the FCC to adopt a policy to reduce telecommunications inequality.

FCC Chairman Reed Hundt is sympathetic. In an April 1995 speech to a school group in Arlington, Va., he said that he "is troubled that 45 million

From Charles S. Clark, "Regulating the Internet," *CQ Researcher*, June 30, 1995. Reprinted by permission.

American children go to 19th-century school buildings every day" at a time when jobs of the future will depend increasingly on telecommunications. The few schools that have been wired have been helped by charities, he noted, "but if we don't adopt it as national policy, it won't happen for all schools."

Also pressing the issue is the ALA, which has launched a campaign called "Americans Can't Wait." In February 1994, the library group passed a resolution recommending to Congress that telecommunications legislation ensure public access to information services during the transition to the new era, specifically "by employing preferential rates, set-asides, least-cost access, universal service contributions and other approaches appropriate for the technology."

> ***"The gap [between information haves and have-nots] is racial as well as economic."***

Congress, as part of the Telecommunications Competition and Deregulation Act [signed into law in February 1996] passed a plan that would require telephone, cable and satellite-communications companies to offer access at affordable rates to schools, clinics and hospitals—using the principle of the universal telephone service fund set up in the 1930s. Advocated by a coalition that includes the National School Boards Association, the National PTA, the Public Broadcasting Service and the major teachers' unions, it was pushed by Sens. Olympia J. Snowe, R-Maine, and John D. Rockefeller IV, D-W.Va. "The market doesn't work in places where you have a low population density," Snowe said during a committee markup. "If companies can't make money in rural areas, they won't serve rural areas."

Drawbacks of Universal Service Plans

Opponents, among them Sen. John Ashcroft, R-Mo., warned that the plan would create an entitlement that would grow unrestrained, while others called it a "tax" on the telephone companies. In a paper on universal service, J. Gregory Sidak of the American Enterprise Institute and Robert W. Crandall of the Brookings Institution said it would be better to let advertisers pay for the information highway and save government efforts for policies that promote competition to keep costs down. An "on ramp" to the information highway may be of little use in areas with poor schools, low literacy rates or high unemployment, the scholars pointed out.

The term "universal service" in the context of the Internet is almost irrelevant, says Tony Rutkowski, executive director of the Internet Society. "Most of the cost is in the end terminal. Does this mean that every user gets a Cray [supercomputer]? Does that mean everyone gets a free course on how to set it up and use it? This isn't the phone, where you pick up and stick it on your ear—there are significant skills required."

There is a difference between universal access and universal service, notes

Edward J. Black, president of the Computer and Communications Industry Association. "We're nervous that service could mean huge subsidies and investments for our members. We support FCC price caps to provide incentives to work with local school districts and hospitals to provide them special access. But direct subsidies drain resources from the public and private sector that may not be needed."

The goal of universality also gets into complicated cross-subsidies. Just as urban, business and long-distance telephone users have long subsidized rural, residential and local users, Internet users in heavily trafficked areas help defray the higher long-distance phone and access charges required in sparsely populated areas.

Any solution also will have to factor in the increasingly competing interests of the telephone companies (regional and long-distance) and the cable television industry as they vie for the opportunities to service private homes in the transmission of broadcast, text, audio, video and graphic data for entertainment and communications.

Can Universal Access Be Ensured?

"The critical question in the Internet's architecture is whether people will have access to all data services and all digital transportation," says Daniel J. Weitzner, deputy director of the Center for Technology and Democracy. "I'm confident that the private sector will deliver video programming because there's lots of money in that. I'm less confident about low-cost, high-bandwidth [high capacity] Internet access. It would be a mistake to try to solve the universal service problem all at once because in 10 years the Internet may be using wireless or satellite technology. It's always a moving target."

Many in the industry and in the Republican-controlled Congress say the best hope for universal access is a deregulated telecommunications industry. "No one ever promised it would be free, but we've been seeing 20–40 percent annual decreases in the cost of technology," says Michael Roberts, a vice-president of Educom, a consortium of colleges and universities offering information-science programs. "Families currently paying $70 a month for cable and phone service could soon get broadband connectivity [to the information highway] for less than $100 a month."

Jeffrey Chester, executive director of the Center for Media Education, rejects the arguments for turning the industry loose. "Access may seem inexpensive now, but the services will be charging more later," he says. "We want to make sure there's no electronic caste system, that every child and school has the access and the ability to manipulate information. There will be incredible resistance from the companies, but there will be a strong public backlash against the members of Congress who vote for this deregulation bill after everyone's phone and cable bills start creeping up."

Universal Access to E-mail Should Be Guaranteed

by Max Frankel

About the author: *Max Frankel is a columnist for the* New York Times Magazine.

It doesn't quite have the ring of John F. Kennedy's vow, in 1961, to land a man on the moon "before this decade is out." But you'd think a President or candidate for President would by now have hurled a similar challenge, with the promise of raising the nation's literacy, its computer skills and its technical prowess: E-mail for All by 2010!

The Power of E-mail

As millions of Americans already know, E-mail is electronic mail that can be sent by anyone with a computer and telephone to everyone similarly equipped, anywhere on earth, almost instantaneously, at virtually no cost. It is by far the most popular feature of the Internet, that amorphous network of computer networks. E-mail's digital messages can be coolly deliberate, like a letter, or warmly spontaneous, like a phone call. They can be sent at any hour and read at the receiver's convenience. They can be addressed to a single person or simultaneously to thousands—thousands chosen by the sender for some shared interest or thousands who asked for a certain type of mail.

Although E-mail will eventually carry moving pictures and oral messages, it is now mostly written—typed, to be precise, on keyboards. Its messages are sliced up and wrapped inside small electronic packets, all of which pick their way along the best available Internet routes to an electronic postal station, where they reassemble and wait in storage for an addressee—like frankel@times.com—to check in to read them. E-mail travels as fast as a fax but arrives in much more versatile form. It can be long or short, studied, searched or skimmed, instantly answered or copied, relayed, edited or destroyed.

E-mail lets you court a lover, proclaim a credo, organize a rally or circulate a recipe. City Hall can use it to schedule trash collections; politicians can use it to

From Max Frankel, "The Moon, This Time Around," *New York Times Magazine*, May 5, 1996.

take a poll. E-mail can order groceries or offer clothing discounts to selected customers. It is certain to become a vital new instrument of commerce and the creator of vibrant electronic communities.

But like conventional telephone and postal service, E-mail will never fulfill its social and commercial promise until it is universal. The more people it can reach, the greater its value to all. The already visible danger is that E-mail will become the preserve of the affluent and educated classes, bypassing large segments of the population—much as paper mail and telephones once bypassed rural America. Now, as then, the market alone seems unable at first to serve its own best interest.

Government Should Subsidize Development of E-mail

It took a decree of Congress to require the Postal Service "to bind the Nation together through the personal, educational, literary and business correspondence of the people . . . in all areas and . . . all communities." As a result, paper mail became a powerful stimulus to road building, railroading and aviation. Similarly, governments imposed universal service on telephone companies, requiring them to overcharge urban customers so as to subsidize the extension of phone lines to far-flung rural areas.

That mail and phone services can now be profitably privatized and deregulated is not an argument against government intervention and leadership. On the contrary, it is proof of the value of government incubation.

"Like conventional telephone and postal service, E-mail will never fulfill its social and commercial promise until it is universal."

A Rand study, with research supported by the Markle Foundation, concluded that in the foreseeable future the free market is likely to deliver E-mail to only half of America. Without a government-led drive toward universality, some E-mail systems may prove to be incompatible with others. And without induced subsidies, perhaps from Internet access fees, the computer industry may never produce the inexpensive technologies that would enable television sets, telephones and computer games to bring E-mail into the home. Interim subsidies and technologies would also be needed if less-affluent citizens are to get their E-mail outside the home, in apartment lobbies, libraries and schools.

Universal E-mail Will Promote Further Computer Uses

There appear to be no technical barriers to achieving universal E-mail once that goal has been proclaimed. Indeed, experiments in a few specially wired communities show that E-mail arouses people's interest in other computer services. In Blacksburg, Va., it has stimulated many to learn more complicated computer skills, to use the Internet for more sophisticated transactions and to create two dozen Net-related businesses.

House Speaker Newt Gingrich was not nearly as "nutty" as he thought when he mused out loud about subsidizing laptops for poor ghetto kids. But he was only scoring debating points and soon abandoned his own insight about how computers threaten to further divide American society.

If political leaders would reflect on the subject, they would recognize a vast constituency of the computerless and computer-challenged. They would recall the rich history of conservatives as well as liberals using government to advance and enlarge the nation's communications and transportation industries. They would summon Microsoft's Bill Gates and I.B.M.'s Lou Gerstner and the other titans of technology who so often deplore our inadequate schooling and seek their commitment to universal E-mail. The computer companies and their charities need to be challenged to underwrite cheaper terminals, to recycle older terminals and to invent pay terminals, like pay phones, for public spaces. They should be asked to consider charging modest fees for profitable private uses of the Internet—a governmental offspring—to subsidize the Net's penetration of every community.

President Kennedy, of course, could invoke the specter of Sputnik and cold war divisions to urge a race against the Russians to the moon. But he set a loftier goal than missile superiority. "Now it is time to take longer strides," he said, "time for a great new American enterprise." We face the more abstract specter of technological partition, a society of computer elites and illiterates drifting apart and losing touch. And we, too, could use a great new enterprise. E-mail for all won't guarantee how well we speak to one another, but it can keep us talking and growing richer together.

Minority Communities Should Be Guaranteed Access to the Internet

by River Ginchild

About the author: *River Ginchild is a civil rights attorney and a member of the community advisory group for the Berkeley Public Library's Internet Project. She is the founder of the Digital Sojourn website at http://www.digitalsojourn.org.*

You can now confidently say "Welcome to the planet" to anyone who has not heard of the Internet. Nearly every household in the country has been bombarded by shrink-wrapped diskettes and CDs offering "free trial access" to the Net, as it's commonly called. Yet in spite of the heavy media coverage of online culture and the business world's newfound obsession with Internet-related companies and activities, fewer than 10 percent of North Americans actually have any kind of meaningful access to the Net. The Internet may be the main component of the information superhighway, but making the conversion from what is now a limited-access road to a true public-access thoroughfare will require some work.

Private Party or Public Revolution?

Understanding the language of the Net and being able to utilize its material are rapidly becoming part of a new basic survival literacy. Every field of employment has been changed by computers and computer-mediated communication. However, telecommunications-industry marketing is primarily geared toward "early adapters"—those who can easily and readily purchase its products and services. In fact, the average annual income of "Net households" is approximately $60,000. According to a study by analyst Kofi Asiedu Ofori, electronic redlining (i.e., bypassing poor communities) "will contribute to the economic decline of impoverished city neighborhoods and create isolated islands of 'information have-nots.'" A 1995 study by the Rand Corporation stated that with-

From River Ginchild, "Caught in the Web," *Third Force*, July/August 1996.

out government intervention to close the widening gap, the nation will soon be experiencing "information apartheid."

At the moment the Net is still largely a reserve for the early adapters and too many among the status quo don't yet see a need to push for universal access. During a panel on universal access at the Ethics of the Internet Conference in Berkeley, Calif., the question "Aren't you afraid that multiculturalism [on the Net] will slow us down?" was shamelessly posed by a member of the audience. At that moment I knew that I (one of two people of African descent in an audience of approximately 150) wanted to be a force in bringing more people like me on line.

Slipping Through the Cracks

The cost of being on line is a major factor in the underrepresentation of some communities on the Net, but the lack of relevant information on the Net contributes to the lack of participation. According to the Rand study, approximately 13 percent of African American, Latino and Native American households have computers, compared to 31 percent of white and 37 percent of Asian American households.

While race and ethnicity as indicators of on-line access have remained constant in the last several years, income and educational status are by far the best indicators. "There is good news and bad news," says Art McGee, coordinator of the African Network of the Institute for Global Communications. "There is an explosion of people of color on line, but there are many who are slipping through the cracks. These are the people who have much more than technology missing in their lives." McGee says he dreams of a future in which technology will be used for communication between African peoples throughout the world, free of the media filters that currently prevent us working together.

Countering the commercial focus of many areas of cyberspace are some exciting telecommunications projects focusing on social and economic justice issues. The Women's Economic Agenda Project (WEAP) in Oakland, Calif., is launching the Women and Technology Program to provide women with computer education and training and to involve grassroots leadership in community revitalization. The Berkeley Macintosh Users Group (BMUG), which is "in the business of giving away information," started a Computer Placement Program, in which they give donated computers to low-income families and offer follow-up training and technical assistance.

> ***"The cost of being on line is a major factor in the underrepresentation of some communities on the Net."***

Randy Ross, a consultant and member of the Smithsonian Institution's National Museum of the American Indian Information/Technology Committee, sees a parallel between Custer's 19th-century raid of the Black Hills and the "elite techno-barons of the end of the 20th century." Ross, a South Dakotan, warns that privatizing the electronic world is likely to result in high-cost access in rural areas. He urges that demonstration projects be deployed in these underserved communities. One example is the way the Native American Public Telecommunications Company has worked with Native Nations to come up with recommendations for ways to get Native Americans on the Net, such as local community networks serving rural communities.

Networks for Communities of Color

LatinoNet is a telecommunications network that primarily serves the Latino community's nonprofit sector, but America Online refused to allow the network to operate a "public area" on AOL, according to Ana Montes, a former LatinoNet systems administrator, "because they felt that we could not generate enough on-line time from our members."

"It was not enough that we got a lot of people to sign on," she said. "We do not encourage our members to spend a lot of time on line with any service. We educate them on how to use the Internet effectively to get what they need and to use it as a vehicle of empowerment. Our slogan is 'get on, get in, do what you need to do and get off.'" When Montes asked why AOL did not expand into Latin America, she was basically told that the corporation "did not believe that the technology was there yet, or enough users to guarantee high profits."

"While race and ethnicity as indicators of on-line access have remained constant, . . . income and educational status are by far the best indicators."

The idea of "no taxation without information" sparked the creation of Austin Free-Net according to its executive director, Sue Beckwith. While the idea of a free network had been floating around Austin, Texas' digerati for a while, lack of time and funding prevented its realization. In 1995 the city committed funding to start the Free-Net when it recognized that many residents were being shut out of civic participation on line. The project's goal is to have Internet access in all public libraries, public-housing learning centers, job training centers and even barber shops in order to involve traditionally underserved communities. Currently, the city's World Wide Web site is updated daily with information on proposed ordinances and schedules for public hearings and city meetings. Residents' excitement for the program is indicated by the more than 100 community volunteers the project has attracted in its first year.

Use It or Lose It

Despite these progressive efforts it is likely that low-income people will be riding coach on the Net for a while longer. The older-model computers and modems that many community and nonprofit groups operate may be adequate for E-mail but are often not equipped to process the graphics, video and sound features available on the World Wide Web.

The reality is that universal access won't truly be attained unless and until every community is equipped with the technology to produce, create and disseminate information, not merely to passively consume it. Rates and equipment must be made affordable and training readily available to productively apply the technology. Once this is achieved we must continually redefine access as the technology advances.

Everyone, whether on line or not, can contribute to the goal of universal access. If you have skills, share them! Invite people to your home or office and give a demonstration. If you are not connected yet, visit your local public library. Many have computers that allow patrons to access the Internet. Nonprofit groups can get connected with volunteers with expertise in both hardware and software through San Francisco–based CompuMentor, which has affiliate projects in Chicago; Boston; Schenectady, N.Y.; New Orleans and Bellevue, Wash. We all can work with progressive media organizations to assure universal access.

Once you are connected, produce your own content! Setting up a Web site or a discussion group is not rocket science. I set up a site called Digital Sojourn because I wanted to see a place for myself and other women of African descent on the Web. I had only seen one or two other pages set up by Black women when I put my first page up in June 1995. The World Wide Web is still overwhelmingly white and male, but every day there are more people of color on line creating exciting material. I did it. You can do it.

"It is likely that low-income people will be riding coach on the Net for a while longer."

Subsidies for Universal Access Should Not Be Expanded

by Peter Pitsch

About the author: *Peter Pitsch is the president of Pitsch Communications, a telecommunications consulting firm. He is an adjunct fellow at the Hudson Institute in Washington, D.C., and a former research director of the Federal Communications Commission.*

Author's note: Although the Telecommunications Act of 1996 differs in important regards from the Markey-Fields bill referenced in this viewpoint, it requires the Federal Communications Commission to address the issues surrounding the definition and reform of universal service that are analyzed below.

Members of Congress and the Clinton administration are seeking to mandate subsidized access to the much ballyhooed information superhighway. Just what this new infrastructure would look like is not clear. Nevertheless, legislation sponsored by Reps. Edward Markey (D., Mass.) and Jack Fields (R., Texas) seeks to expand universal service policies for telephones to include new services such as interactive television. In addition, Vice President Al Gore proposed that telecommunications companies provide subsidized access to public schools and libraries. This is necessary, Mr. Gore said, to prevent the creation of a society of "information haves and have-nots."

These proposals are well-intentioned. But at best they are premature and fail to come to grips with the real challenges facing universal service today. At worst, they could delay the implementation of new interactive services and set back the telecommunications revolution.

Telephone service in the U.S. is now virtually universal. As of November 1993 over 94% of U.S. households had a telephone and nearly 96% had access to one. Under current universal service policies, subsidies run to local telephone

From Peter Pitsch, "Disconnect the Universal Subsidy," *Wall Street Journal*, April 4, 1994.

companies from long-distance providers and to rural local telephone companies from larger, lower-cost local telephone companies. Even though monthly local service prices are roughly the same, the average access-line costs for the smallest, primarily rural, local telephone companies are more than twice as much as those for the Regional Bell Operating Companies. Thus long-distance callers, urban users and businesses pay significantly higher rates and residential callers, especially in rural areas, pay below-cost rates.

These universal service policies have been justified on two grounds. First, most Americans regard telephone service as a necessity, if only for health and safety reasons. Second, the benefits of subsidizing access for rural and low-income households may outweigh the costs. Encouraging rural users to buy telephone services increases the value of the service to all other callers who now have more users to call or be called by.

Internet Services Are Not Necessities

Neither of these rationales justifies the proposed expansion of universal service to include new digital services. By no stretch of the imagination can the added benefits of interactive video service, for example, be regarded as necessities. The objectives of health and safety are met by the telephone system. Nor does the economic rationale for telephone universality apply here. For the foreseeable future much of the benefit of the digital network to individual customers will likely come from their ability to access large, centralized databases, not other subscribers.

The new services may sound wonderful, but the prospects for individual technologies are highly uncertain. Encumbering these already risky endeavors with premature universal service obligations heightens that risk and discourages rather than fosters investment and innovation. We should not create a significant new regulatory entitlement for such things as interactive video services before we have a better understanding of the economics and demand for them.

Once these services are proven, consumers can weigh the practical benefits of each offering. Market forces will then lead to the rapid spread of the most popular services. It bears noting, in this regard, that unsubsidized broadcast television, now reaching more than 98% of all households, is more "universal" than subsidized telephone service.

> ***"[Universal service proposals] could delay the implementation of new interactive services and set back the telecommunications revolution."***

One thing that is now certain is that the information superhighway will not be cost-free. This fact apparently escapes the administration and other proponents of requiring telecom firms to provide subsidized access to schools and libraries. It is not enough to criticize "corporate greed" if in the end other customers would pay.

Ideally these decisions could be made and funded at the local level. When there is a track record, local governments could decide for themselves whether the benefits of "wiring" schools and libraries outweigh the benefits of various alternatives, such as raising teachers' salaries or adding science facilities and computers. At a minimum, before mandating that companies fund access (and possibly monthly service) for all of America's schools and libraries, we should determine how successful the new service will be. The costs of such a program would be more manageable if the base of paying customers is large.

Allow More Competition

Rather than expanding universal service, policy makers should focus on adapting existing universal service policies to meet the profound challenges that may be presented by local competition. Once unthinkable, widespread competition in local telephone markets now seems possible because of breakthroughs in fiber-optic and wireless technologies. But while competition holds great promise for all telecommunications consumers, it will eliminate the phone companies' ability to overcharge high-margin customers, who currently subsidize rural and high-cost users. This may undermine today's universal service policies.

"We should not create a significant new regulatory entitlement for such things as interactive video services."

The Markey-Fields bill would address this universal service problem by creating a panel of federal-state regulators to establish specific and predictable mechanisms for universal service. While reconfiguring current requirements will require Solomon-like wisdom, two guidelines seem clear.

First, instead of increasing subsidies, we should reduce them. Recent experience shows that this wouldn't jeopardize universal telephone service. Subscribership levels have gone up despite rate increases, and now low-cost options for low-volume users are widespread. In the 1980s, reductions in the long-distance subsidy for local companies were a huge success: Household penetration rates increased a full three percentage points; long-distance prices were reduced approximately 40%; and long-distance calling burgeoned. Further reductions in this subsidy would produce even more long-distance price reductions. Note that rural callers make more long-distance calls on average than do urban customers. Even many low-income customers could benefit. One study found that low-income customers paid over 60% of their monthly bill for long-distance service.

Second, if existing programs that subsidize local phone companies directly remain necessary, they should be retooled to help only truly high-cost areas. We should scale back existing programs, such as the FCC-created Universal Service Fund, that allow local phone companies to start requesting subsidies when their costs exceed 115% of the national average. Besides discouraging efficient operation, this program covers too many companies—about 675 now qualify. Programs like this should be made as competitive as possible. One way to achieve this would be for the government to hold reverse auctions to determine whether other companies might be willing to make services available at a lower level of subsidy.

Unpaved Superhighway

The information superhighway is far from being paved. Segments may be made from fiber-optic and coaxial cable. Other parts may use subscribers' existing copper wires. Still other parts may use radio waves. Increasingly it looks like consumers may be able to choose between parallel roads. With all this uncertainty, policy makers should take care not to undermine these developments with premature talk about universality and subsidized access. This will only distort investment.

What we do know is that competition in local telecommunications markets will require carefully crafted changes to existing universal service policies. This may not be as glamorous as working on the information superhighway, but it is where policy makers can do the American public the most good right now.

Minority Communities Are Not Being Denied Access to the Internet

by Robert Wright

About the author: *Robert Wright is a contributing editor for the* New Republic*, a weekly liberal newsmagazine.*

The structure of the data superhighway is "the civil rights issue of the twenty-first century." This opinion comes from the United Church of Christ, part of a coalition of liberal groups that landed on the front page of the *New York Times* with a study alleging "electronic redlining." The study looked at neighborhoods where the Baby Bells are testing fiber-optic "video dial tone" service. It sensed a recurring theme of affluence and whiteness and concluded that the superhighway is bypassing the underprivileged. The study's sponsors, among them the NAACP, want "anti-redlining" rules in the epic telecommunications legislation now forming in Congress. [The Telecommunications Competition and Deregulation Act eventually signed into law in February 1996 requires communications companies to provide information services to all areas of the country at affordable rates.]

There is certainly much to dislike in the emerging data superhighway (including the name—hereafter: the "dataway"). And there are things about it that will indeed harm the urban underclass. But whether "redlining" is among them, and warrants a liberal crusade, is another question.

Different Visions of the Information Highway

The issue turns partly on which of the two basic visions of the dataway you buy. One is the "cornucopia of edification" vision: in the world of tomorrow, you will download interactive cello lessons, join in a global seminar on arms control, take a virtual tour of Incan ruins. In the alternative scenario (the "cornucopia of narcotics" vision), the dataway is a tool by which corporations will pump the

From Robert Wright, "TRB from Washington: Low Fiber," *New Republic*, June 27, 1994. Reprinted by permission of the *New Republic*; ©1994, The New Republic, Inc.

contents of Blockbuster video into the nerve endings of Americans so long as they retain enough sentience to interactively pay their bills. Plus home shopping.

The first vision seems to be assumed by the authors of the redlining report, and is held also by dataway boosters in Congress. Unfortunately, it's the second vision that drives the "market forces" these boosters would unleash to build the dataway. (The bills in Congress would free the Bells, cable companies, MCI, etc. to compete in everything—local and long distance, voice and video. Since the presumably hot video market requires broad bandwidth, these companies would be enticed into laying fiber, thus building the dataway. Of course, barring government constraint, they'll wire the most lucrative areas first; hence "redlining.")

Now, if the dataway works as it should (inscrutable technical translation: if we build a "switched, open network"), the two visions can coexist. People will face nearly infinite options, via data vendors large and small, high-minded and low, and will be free to choose their fate. The question behind the redlining debate is: What choices would underclass teenagers make? Virtual calculus or Mortal Kombat?

First of all, teenagers in general will tend to take fluff and trash over education. Parents, too. In *any* neighborhood, somewhere around 95 percent of any dataway subsidy would go for light entertainment. (An anti-redlining law amounts to a subsidy to lay fiber in economically unattractive areas, financed by an implicit tax on fiber in upscale areas.) Second, if the "underclass" label is accurate, the numbers will be even worse in the inner city. The term connotes a culture in which the values and aspirations absorbed by children don't foster efficient self-improvement.

"In* any *neighborhood, somewhere around 95 percent of any dataway subsidy would go for light entertainment."

Of course, there are stories about inner-city kids who would be great scholars were scholarship not ridiculed by their peers. Maybe some covert virtual calculus is just what they need. But there's also the perverse possibility that the dataway will pull some underclass kids further under. During the heyday of broadcast television, video was a unifier, a lifeline to the mainstream. The dataway will be a fragmenter—like cable T.V., only more so. It will segregate us into micro-communities, envelop us in our distinctive obsessions. Right now the obsessions of many underclass teenagers aren't good.

Not Rich vs. Poor, but Urban vs. Rural

Even if being left off the dataway would be a net handicap for the underclass, it's not clear that we'd have a big problem on our hands. There is some doubt about the redlining report's central suggestion that redlining truly will be a lasting urban phenomenon. Granted, showcase fiber-optic experiments take place mostly in well-coiffed suburbs; and, granted, cable companies have often entered inner cities only under political pressure. But many of those companies then found that people there not only subscribe to cable, but pay for premium channels. A large fraction of their small entertainment dollar goes to home video. The market will bring fiber to the Upper West Side faster than to Harlem, but maybe not much faster.

"The market will bring fiber to the Upper West Side faster than to Harlem, but maybe not much faster."

Redlining is more likely in the country, where people live far apart. Historically, the Baby Bells—protected monopolies committed by law to provide "universal" (broadly affordable) service—have met that goal by cross-subsidy. Artificially high urban rates permitted artificially low rural rates. But as the Bells are exposed to competition, artificial rates will become untenable. In the new world, many rural residents won't get fiber without specific government help.

Whether or not such help is in order, the bills in Congress would provide some, in the form of an expanded universal service fund. The money will come from all corporate players—in effect, a tax on dataway construction. Presumably, rural interests will try to steer the proceeds toward rural fiber while civil rights groups (judging by the redlining report) try to steer it toward urban fiber.

Money Could Be Better Spent

The inner city definitely needs the money, but are living rooms really the place where it will most help the underclass? How about the public schools instead? We all know how badly they spend money, but surely they don't waste ninety-five cents of each dollar, as an anti-redlining subsidy probably would.

The spending needn't stop at free dataway hookups for schools (already an easy and popular sound bite). Urban schools also need computers, books, teachers, desks, walls. They're a disaster area, the most vivid disgrace in American government.

The fiberization of America brings that rare and sublime moment in public policy: the birth of a cash cow. We can tax fiber without any group distinctly feeling much pain. Of course, this would slow dataway construction. But how tragic is that? Whatever its redeeming features, the dataway will encourage cultural division at a time of divisiveness. And let's face it: it will probably increase income inequality, too. Presumably more kids will use the dataway educationally in Hyde Park [an upper-class neighborhood in Chicago] (if only under parental pressure) than in the Robert Taylor Homes [a public housing project]. With or without redlining laws, and with or without redlining, the dataway will bring economic benefits to Americans in inverse proportion to their need for the benefits. Nationwide construction delays aren't something that liberals need mourn.

A heavy fiber tax, given mainly to inner-city schools, would be an uphill battle in Congress. But at least it's a goal worthy of the civil rights movement. Subsidizing teenagers who watch T.V. is not.

Chapter 5

Will Computers Transform Education?

Computers and Education: An Overview

by Christopher Conte

About the author: *Christopher Conte is a freelance writer in Washington, D.C.*

The idea of linking schools to the computer network known as the Internet has become one of the hottest education topics of the 1990s. President Clinton has said the U.S. should set a national goal of connecting every school to the information superhighway by the year 2000. "I want to get the children of America hooked on education through computers," Clinton said in a speech in California September 21, 1995, adding, "we must make technological literacy a standard."

The Cost of Computers for Schools

But Clinton's networking goal almost certainly is beyond reach. Currently, just 3 percent of the nation's elementary, middle and high school classrooms have Internet connections, and only about 16 percent of teachers use the Internet or computer-based communication services like America Online, CompuServe or Prodigy, according to the Denver research firm Quality Education Data, Inc. Linking the remaining classrooms could cost $30 billion or more, plus at least $5 billion in annual operating expenses. Currently, schools spend under $3 billion of their $249 billion annual budgets on all forms of technology, according to McKinsey & Co., a New York–based consulting firm.

Some critics question whether the current fascination with computer networking is blinding us to more pressing needs. "Our schools face serious problems, including overcrowded classrooms, teacher incompetence and lack of security," notes Clifford Stoll, author of a popular critique of cyber culture, *Silicon Snake Oil: Second Thoughts on the Information Highway*. "Computers address none of these problems. They're expensive, quickly become obsolete and drain scarce capital budgets."

Still, the idea of bringing computer networking to schools has captivated many policy-makers, educators and parents. In the process, it has spawned a vi-

From Christopher Conte, "Networking the Classroom," *CQ Researcher*, October 20, 1995. Reprinted by permission.

brant dialogue about the way classrooms function, the relationship between schools and other institutions and, ultimately, even what students should be expected to learn.

The push to connect classrooms draws much of its force from a vision that computer networks could serve as catalysts for fundamental reform of education. In the traditional classroom, teachers are the focal point of activity. They transmit an established body of knowledge to students, who are judged by their ability to absorb and repeat those basic skills and facts. But in the new, reform model, students assume more responsibility for setting their own educational goals and then develop skills to seek, sift and analyze information in pursuit of these objectives.

A Change in the Role of Teachers

As for teachers, they "change from being the repository of all knowledge to being guides or mentors who help students navigate through the information made available by technology and interactive communication," says the National Academy of Sciences. "They help students gather and organize information, judge its value and decide how to present it to others."

The idea of "student-centered" or "inquiry-based" learning traces its roots back at least to 18th-century philosophers like Rousseau. But it has gained added impetus as the economy has evolved from the mass production model of the 20th century to a 21st century "information age" model. As a growing number of educators and economists see it, the traditional classroom, with its strong central authority and its emphasis on training students to take orders and perform narrow tasks, may have prepared children adequately for work in 20th-century factories. But it can't impart the skills they need in the workplace of the 21st century, where there's a premium on workers who are flexible, creative, self-directed and able to solve problems collaboratively.

Besides, analysts argue, knowledge is changing so rapidly that teaching an established body of facts is of little value. It's more important now, educators say, to give students the skills to go on learning throughout their lives. "In 1850, it took about 50 years to double the world's knowledge base," notes Frank Withrow, director of learning technologies for the Council of Chief State School Officers. "Today, it takes only a little more than a year. The way we store, retrieve and use information is vastly different in the information age. . . . The American work force does not need 'knowers,' it needs 'learners.'"

> ***"The push to connect classrooms draws much of its force from a vision that computer networks could serve as catalysts for fundamental reform of education."***

In the early days of computers in classrooms, critics worried that technology would undermine the role of schools in socializing children. But networking advocates say that linking computers actually increases social interaction and collaboration. "The Internet is much, much more than just a vast library of information: It is also a community . . . a gathering place . . . where you can find experts on almost any topic . . . and share your expertise with the world," says the Online Internet Institute, one of various groups that introduce teachers to computer networking. "This is a place where collaboration and synergy occurs, where the results and benefits you experience far exceed the sum of their individual parts."

"Networking advocates say that linking computers actually increases social interaction and collaboration."

Further, advocates argue that computer networking, by conveying the printed word electronically, combines the speed and immediacy of the oral tradition with the opportunity for more considered communication associated with the printed word. And they contend that computer-based communication allows just enough distance that artificial social barriers—including the segregation of children from the rest of society (and even each other) in age-graded classrooms—lose their relevance.

"Kids need lots of interaction with adults," says Mary Ellen Verona, a computer sciences teacher at Montgomery Blair High School in Silver Springs, Md., and principal investigator for the Maryland Virtual High School Project, which seeks to link schools for collaborative learning projects. With networking, she argues, "school becomes part of the real world. It's no longer an age ghetto."

Keeping Children Interested in Learning

Instant communications have become so much a part of American life, she adds, that it is becoming increasingly difficult for schools to operate without them: "You can't expect to keep kids interested with five- or 10-year-old textbooks when they're exposed to instant information on CNN and computers at home."

One thing is clear: Computer networking has unleashed tremendous enthusiasm in schools that have it. "My curriculum has never been so up-to-date, so exciting for me," says Patricia Weeg, who teaches at Delmar (Md.) Elementary School. Using KIDLINK, a grassroots project that has drawn 37,000 students together, Weeg's students have established computer "keypals" in Finland, Russia, Tasmania, Japan, Brazil and elsewhere. They have talked about the pyramids with an Egyptian schoolgirl named Mariam, learned from kids in Alaska about life in a remote village and taken a "virtual tour" of the Thames River with a British teacher.

"Are we linked to a larger teaching and learning community?" asks Weeg. "You bet we are! . . . In the global classroom, the curriculum is a 'living' curriculum with real people—not textbooks—feeding our desire to learn and explore."

For many teachers, originating communications is at least as important as receiving them. Mary O'Haver, a teacher at Fairland Elementary School, near Montgomery Blair, has turned her fifth-grade social studies class into a veritable publishing empire. Her students have used desktop publishing skills to prepare handsome autobiographical newspapers. On their Web page, they have presented commemorative stamps on the Bill of Rights and important figures in American history. Several, like Christine Brewer, who prepared a report on Pocahontas, have received e-mail from far-flung readers.

Joyce Brunsvold, a Fairland reading teacher, says children are more motivated when they know they're actually communicating with people beyond school. "Kids know that parents and teachers are going to say 'Good job,'" she notes. "But when a total stranger sends e-mail commenting on something you wrote, it means a lot more." In addition, Brunsvold says, children find it easier to write and edit on the computer—and hence, do more of both.

Computers Offer Teachers a New Tool

Being connected has a pronounced impact on teachers, too. O'Haver spends relatively little time lecturing or policing behavior. And she has exchanged ideas about teaching and even conducted some joint classes with teachers in Tasmania and British Columbia. She also plugs in to MDK-12, an on-line network for teachers hosted by the University of Maryland. In short, networking has banished the classroom teacher's traditional isolation. "Who would have thought this electronic device could bring me so many friends?" asks O'Haver.

For O'Haver, part of the process of lesson planning is searching the Internet for new connections for her students. One day she stumbled upon Monarch Watch, a research project launched by University of Kansas entomologists. Using the Internet, they have enlisted an estimated 20,000 students nationwide to help track the annual migration of monarch butterflies. Students catch monarchs, tag them and report on any tagged butterflies they find.

The idea of grade schoolers participating in real research and learning from actual scientists is almost as captivating as monarch butterflies themselves. But as yet there is no agreement that it's worth the investment that would be required to achieve it.

> ***"One thing is clear: Computer networking has unleashed tremendous enthusiasm in schools that have it."***

"Schools are faced with an enormous price tag, but they're looking at shrinking state budgets and an attack on federal investment in education," notes Michelle Richards, federal networks advocate for the National School Boards Association. "The only recourse they have, other than cutting existing programs, is to raise local taxes—and most communities aren't willing to do that."

Whether advocates of networking can build the sustained public support needed to connect schools depends, in large part, on the answers to some basic questions.

Does computer networking really enhance learning? There is no simple answer. Hundreds of studies suggest that computers can be effective teaching tools, though not dramatically better than other technologies or traditional instructional methods. But most of this research has focused on earlier, self-contained uses of computers, and therefore may be of limited value to the current debate over networking.

> ***"The impact of computers and computer networking on higher-order skills is intensely debated."***

Moreover, many of the analyses suffer serious methodological flaws. In a 1985 review, Richard Clark, an education professor at the University of Southern California–Los Angeles, found that researchers frequently failed to distinguish the effect of computers in the classroom from that of the teachers delivering the instruction. Much of the supposed beneficial impact of computers disappeared, he said, when the teacher or instructional method were held constant.

Clark also reported that computers generally were credited with having the biggest effect in short-term studies. This suggested that much of the gain associated with computers may have resulted from the novelty of the new technology, rather than some underlying advantage.

"The best current evidence is that media are mere vehicles that deliver instruction, but do not influence student achievement any more than the truck that delivers our groceries causes changes in nutrition," Clark concluded. "Only the content of the vehicle can influence achievement."

What Can Be Taught Through Computers?

In recent years, most educators have come to agree that technology cannot be considered separately from the whole context in which it is used—including, especially, the philosophy and style of individual teachers and schools. "We know that technology may have important contributory effects to learning, but that they are crucially mediated by social practices in the classroom by teachers and students," says Roy D. Pea, an educational researcher at Northwestern University.

Still, technology advocates and education reformers worry that traditional methods for assessing student learning fail to gauge the skills most closely associated with computer networking. While standardized tests and other common assessment tools measure student mastery of discrete skills and factual knowledge, these analysts argue, they don't adequately determine whether students are acquiring such "higher-order" skills as the ability to solve problems, think analytically, synthesize information from diverse sources and communicate effectively.

Perhaps because of the lack of adequate research findings, the impact of computers and computer networking on higher-order skills is intensely debated.

Critics contend that networking can militate against these skills by undermining the relationship between teachers and students. As they see it, many teachers who use the Internet in the classroom confuse access to information with real knowledge, and mistakenly put the capacity to compile data ahead of the ability to analyze and understand it.

"Isolated facts don't make an education," writes Stoll. "Meaning doesn't come from data alone. Creative problem solving depends on context, interrelationships and experience. . . . And only human beings can teach the connections between things."

Some research, however, does support the claim that networking, if properly used, helps students develop higher-order skills. In one study, Margaret Riel, a professor at the University of California at San Diego, found that fourth-graders in California, Hawaii, Mexico and Alaska who participated in an on-line news service called "Computer Chronicles" showed marked improvement in reading and writing skills compared with other students. Riel concluded that editing other kids' writing is more effective than looking for one's own mistakes, and that students felt more comfortable editing the work of distant peers than that of their own classmates.

Computers May Enhance Writing Skills

Another study by Riel suggested that students perform better when they're given authentic tasks rather than make-work assignments. In the study, judges were given two sets of papers written by Israeli students—some written for a student network and others for teachers. Without knowing for whom the papers were written, the judges found the writing done for peers was more substantive, supported more effectively by details, used less slang, had more complex constructions and contained fewer errors.

The Software Publishers Association reported similar positive evaluations of the National Geographic Society's Kids Network, in which fourth- and fifth-graders collected data on acid rain and shared their data on-line with remote classes. The students showed substantial gains in the ability to organize, represent and interpret data, plus increased understanding of geography and environmental issues.

"While considerable work is being done to develop newer methods for assessing student performance, it may not be easy to sell the public on them."

While considerable work is being done to develop newer methods for assessing student performance, it may not be easy to sell the public on them. The new measures rely more than standardized tests on subjective evaluations of performance. And like the more complex phenomena they are designed to gauge, newer assessment tools are harder to reduce to simple, quantifiable scores; how, for instance, do you reduce to a single, SAT-type score a student's ability to engage in sustained intellectual inquiry or participate effectively on a team of researchers?

The Belridge School in McKittrick, Calif., learned first-hand about the pressures parents and school administrators can apply for quick, quantifiable results. A few years ago, it invested heavily in computers and software, laser disc players and television-production equipment in an attempt to revamp its curriculum. After acquiring the technology, the school assigned students such challenging and authentic projects as producing their own television news shows and running a computer-based presidential election. But when standardized test scores two years later didn't show any improvement, parents picketed the school and elected a new school board to find a "back-to-the-basics" principal. Computers were removed from students' desks.

Computer Education Is Vital for Students of the Future

by Richard W. Riley

About the author: *Richard W. Riley is the secretary of the U.S. Department of Education.*

Some years ago, a business leader reminded me that the adventurers who set out for the New World were able to smell land long before they caught sight of it. Like those mariners, said this businessman, today's leaders have to be able to "smell the future." They have to be able to think long term and see beyond the horizon. I believe that the future beckons America. It promises rewarding jobs. It offers to diminish the drudgery and toil of daily labor. It opens prospects of abundance and rising standards of living for every American. All of these things are possible if our children are prepared, if they are provided with the tools they need to adjust to new circumstances and changing times. The wealth built by our forebears from coal, steel, oil, concrete, and brawn can be built tomorrow from silicon chips, integrated circuits, digital networks, computers, and raw intelligence.

Revolutionary Inventions

In a larger sense, all of these things are possible because Americans have always understood that the future is not something that simply arrives but something that is created by the actions that we take today to secure our children's tomorrow. Throughout history, the march of human progress has been marked by milestones in science and technology. Gutenberg's creation of movable type in the 15th century laid the foundation for universal literacy. Watts' invention of the steam engine in the 18th century launched the Industrial Revolution. The inventiveness of Bell and Marconi in the 19th and 20th centuries, creating the telephone and radio, helped bring a global village into being.

The United States and the world are now in the midst of an economic and social revolution every bit as sweeping as any that have gone before, one grounded in telecommunications and digital technologies. In the year 2000, when 1995's infants enter school and 1995's eighth graders graduate, these technologies and the national and international infrastructures they make possible will be commonplace. These children must be prepared to make their way in this new age, in this different world. Entering this new environment, the United States will either lead the transformation or it will follow the lead of others. If this generation of Americans has the courage to do for its children what prior generations did for theirs, the possibilities for the United States are limitless.

"It is in the schools that the United States will obtain the greatest returns on its investments in technology."

If this generation does not possess that courage—if it falters, hesitates, and ultimately refuses to open the door to the digital era—global competitors will certainly open the door first, and reap the rewards. And if this transformation is to come to full bloom, it must take root in the nation's schools. For it is in the nation's schools, with their 49 million students and 2.5 million teachers, that the country's future is conceived, created, and secured. And it is in the schools that the United States will obtain the greatest returns on its investments in technology—immediate returns in the form of more productive and rewarding teaching and learning and longer-term benefits of geometric increases in individual and national productivity.

Time to Choose

Education in America is at a critical crossroads. On the one hand, in the past decade parents, educators, legislators, and business and community leaders have worked hard to create a broad-based, bipartisan consensus on how to improve American education. The result of these efforts is the Goals 2000: Educate America Act, passed by Congress and signed into law by President Clinton in 1994. Goals 2000 lays out eight national education goals and creates, for the first time, a national partnership to support community-based school improvement efforts.

On the other hand, the use of technology in American life has exploded in the 1990s, affecting everything from the workplace to the living room. As secretary of education, I have come to believe that it will be possible to provide the kind of quality education for every student outlined in Goals 2000 only if our young people have access to these new technologies and information tools—to computers, networks, CD-ROMs, modems, and the emerging national information infrastructure (NII)—known popularly as the information superhighway.

The information superhighway is a "seamless" web of computers, communications networks, libraries, data bases, and consumer electronics that will put vast amounts of information at our fingertips. Ultimately, it will tie together telephone systems, which already reach 98 percent of households; cable systems, which pass by more than 90 percent of homes; broadcast and radio stations; cellular telephone systems and other wireless networks; satellites already offering programming directly to owners of "dishes" no larger than salad bowls; and enormous information data bases.

Technology can help tailor instruction to the individual needs of students; improve instructional management; support teachers and their professional development; connect student learning with the real world and schools to the home and community; and expand time for learning beyond the traditional school day. We should therefore set for ourselves the goal of providing a learning system that permits all of our people, young and old, to learn whatever they need to, whenever they want to, wherever they choose to. That is to say, the nation should set out to create the kinds of learning institutions it has always wanted and needed—schools that tailor instruction to the specific, individual needs of each student and that encourage students to learn at their own pace and throughout their lives.

Ensuring Access

The principle of free public education—not cheap, not half-priced, not cut-rate, but in its very essence free—for all children is the bedrock of our democracy. Educational institutions, large and small—schools, libraries, literacy centers, early childhood centers, community colleges, and universities—should have total access to and use of services on the information superhighway. There should be "on-ramps" and "off-ramps" to every classroom. If cost limitations or other practical considerations make it impossible to connect the NII with all educational institutions at once, then schools, libraries, and literacy centers should be at the front of the line when public institutions are linked in the decade ahead.

Why at the front of the line? In the coming decade, this nation will have approximately 55.7 million students in public and private schools—7 million more than we have today. A growing proportion of these young people will be Latino and Hispanic, African-American, or new immigrants, many of them low-income and living in communities traditionally poorly served by our schools. Parents understand how important it is that their children learn, all the more so in a technological age. As technology breaks down the walls separating home from school, and as students and parents are connected with distant libraries and classrooms around the globe, community leaders must make sure that no child is left behind.

> ***"It will be possible to provide . . . quality education for every student . . . only if our young people have access to these new technologies and information tools."***

Educators know how valuable technology is to students isolated by geography or challenged by poverty or disability. New satellite and distance learning techniques can bring the best teaching to the most remote home or school. Well-implemented instructional learning systems have produced some spectacular results for low-income children in compensatory (Title I) programs. The same technologies used to train pilots are being used experimentally to teach orthopedically impaired children, most with cerebral palsy, how to operate motorized wheelchairs and negotiate the obstacles that they might find in a typical classroom or busy street.

"Recent disturbing reports suggest that low-income inner-city and rural neighborhoods may be the last ones served by new technologies."

Recent disturbing reports suggest that low-income inner-city and rural neighborhoods may be the last ones served by new technologies. It is no secret that a young person who gets a quality education becomes a more dependable worker, a better citizen, and a stronger consumer. If the nation continues to ignore the educational needs of new students—particularly low-income students—and continues to give them a watered-down curriculum and link up their schools last, it will find itself in an economic bind of the first order. It will have a work force that does not know how to work.

If the United States continues to think short term, as it did in the 1980s, the results are potentially disastrous. Every year, large corporations and small businesses, two- and four-year colleges, and public and private universities spend billions of dollars on remedial education. If the nation does it right the first time, it can eliminate this costly and wasteful need to keep redoing it. To create a well-educated, world-class work force, now is the time to get it right—and get it right the first time. I believe that early investments in education technology will provide handsome long-term economic returns, and that the costs will be returned to all of us, many times over, in the form of lower public assistance costs and greater national productivity.

Getting There

How best to proceed with that investment is a challenging question. Conflicting views on the role of the federal government in education present a problem. The rapidity with which technology is evolving requires attention. The central place of the private sector in technological evolution demands respect. In brief, a strategy for the nation cannot be imposed by the federal government. How do we get from here to there?

Nobody expects the federal government to solve all the problems associated with educational technology. But parents and educators are demanding leadership to see that problems and issues are addressed. Government's role—at all levels, federal, state, and local—is to point people in the right direction and urge them along the road. Officials should use their bully pulpit to define the stakes involved in the education technology debate and encourage public and private leaders to tackle the challenges ahead.

The first thing to understand is that technology is not a cost but an investment. Educators need an investment mentality that is firm, fair, and flexible. That is to say, schools should firmly commit themselves to technology as the wave of the future. Nothing will more quickly defeat the effort to improve learning and school use of technology than half-steps, half-measures, and half-hearted commitment. The strategy is doomed that concludes, "We will put an extra computer here and purchase an extra piece of software there and provide a little extra teacher training elsewhere—as soon as we find a little extra money." As everyone knows, "a little extra money" is hard to find. Much more likely to succeed is a firm strategy based on a clear vision of what is to be accomplished and how school leaders propose to get there.

Policy planning must also be fair. Whether or not schools invest in technology, children from affluent and middle-income families will enjoy access to the latest technologies in their homes—including powerful personal computers and peripheral devices such as CD-ROMs, scanners, printers, modems, and network connections. State and local leaders should insist that schools in the lowest-income neighborhoods be the first to be provided with the latest technologies.

"Schools should firmly commit themselves to technology as the wave of the future."

Finally, although schools should be firm in their commitment to technology and fair in their allocation of it, they must also be flexible in their implementation. The useful lifetime of many of today's technologies is about five to six years. In fact, the power of integrated circuitry is expanding so rapidly that new, cutting-edge computer platforms and affiliated software appear about every 18 months. In the past decade, technology has matured so rapidly that many public schools—like many governments, homes, and firms in the private sector—are already saddled with badly out-of-date equipment. Schools need to be flexible enough to stay abreast of change, not so completely wedded to one way of doing things that they are unable to respond as these technologies mature.

Empowering Teachers

Bringing the full fruits of new technologies to our schools depends on many things. Schools need expanded access to the information highway. They need better tools and educational software. They need independent analyses and trustworthy advice about the benefits of technology. And they need new alliances with the private sector. Above all, our nation needs to do a much better job of developing teachers' professional skills by training them to use new technology effectively. One of the most striking findings to emerge in the U.S. Department of Education's review of developments in technology is that the private sector spends three times as much on technology training as do the nation's schools.

As secretary of education, I have become convinced that the Department of Education's leadership role in this entire area can best be met by tackling the teacher training and professional development issue head on. When all is said and done about access to the information highway, tools and software, research and development, and partnerships with the private sector, I believe that much of what we're aiming for can be summed up in one sentence: By the year 2000, the nation should provide every teacher in the United States with the opportunity to take advantage of first-class training in the latest and most up-to-date technologies available for the classroom.

"The nation should provide every teacher . . . first-class training in the latest and most up-to-date technologies available for the classroom."

It is quite clear that technology offers profound new possibilities not only for learners but also for teachers. Computers and telecommunications can improve the professional working lives of teachers. They can help generate and modify instructional materials. They offer interaction with a wide circle of peers, instantaneous communication with instructional and subject-matter experts, and access to enormous quantities of background and reference materials. They can, in brief, help redefine the teacher's role.

In one sense, the nation owes its teachers nothing less. In another, it owes its students nothing less. But in the final analysis, the nation owes itself and its future nothing less. It is time, once again, for Americans to "smell the future." That future, and all of its promises and possibilities, continues to beckon.

Computers Are a Necessary Resource for Schools

by Reed E. Hundt

About the author: *Reed E. Hundt is the chairman of the Federal Communications Commission.*

Before I was chairman of the Federal Communications Commission, I had a respectable job. I was a school teacher.

Unfortunately, I was not a particularly good school teacher. I say that not with any sense of false modesty. It was definitely not something that I had a gift for, and it takes a gift.

Schools Lack Resources

In addition to my lack of the gift for teaching, I was put in an impossible situation, the type of situation that so many teachers face every day.

This was before the communications revolution and we suffered a major deficit in information technology—we had only books.

Before my first class on the first day, someone came by and gave me 35 textbooks, which I handed out to everyone in class. After a few minutes of calm, the bell rang and everybody except me raced to squeeze through the door simultaneously. After about half had escaped, I realized that they had taken their books with them. However, I had four more classes arriving and was down to 11 books. These did not survive past lunch.

The rest of the year, I taught with purple-stained fingers as I distributed wrinkled mimeo-papers. I had to make up the lessons because I had not even kept one textbook for myself.

It was no fun for those kids to have no books—to have nothing. And I had to go home at night knowing that they were not getting the education they needed.

Today, the children of the kids I taught are in high school. And, relative to what they need, these kids have even less.

They may have a computer in their class—99 percent of all schools do—but it is likely to be so out of date that, even if the classroom had a phone line—

From Reed E. Hundt, "Bring the Revolution Home." Reprinted with permission from *Education Week*, vol. 14, no. 32, May 3, 1995.

which 90 percent of all classrooms do not—the computer could not be used to send electronic mail. We are all in the information age, but those kids are still not being taught basic literacy.

If Horace Mann came back today and walked into any school in America, he would be very proud of what he'd accomplished until he found out that it was almost the 21st century and nothing had changed. It would be disappointing to Horace to find out what's been left out. We have 40 million people in this country who go to work and play and study every day in rooms that might as well be in the 19th century, and you know this. Those are our teachers and our kids.

To begin to solve this problem, it is absolutely essential that every classroom have some link to send and receive information.

When this happens, the hierarchies are going to flatten. More people who do important jobs are going to find that their jobs are re-tailored and they will be in actual contact with students instead of an administration. We're going to find that budgets are going to be freed up and more money is going to be available for actually reducing the size of classrooms.

Parental involvement will change forever if we get communications technology in classrooms. You will find that you are drawing parents in. Every study says you have to have parental involvement to change education. You will give them the tools to be drawn in, and they will pay the commercial companies for their own access.

Schools Need Computer Network Connection

How long is the school day? Everybody in education knows that the school day is not long enough. Kids in this country don't go to school enough. They don't spend enough time learning. These are serious issues. But we cannot expect it to be the case in our current school systems that we raise enough money to make the schools stay open longer, or raise enough money to pay teachers more so that they will stay there more. Those are not possibilities in the real world. What is a possibility is that technology will lengthen the time period for learning, that technology will permit homework and work assignments to be sent over networks to homes. That's why they should call it "homework." Send it to homes and let parents and teachers talk about it with kids in the electronic world.

> ***"We are all in the information age, but those kids are still not being taught basic literacy."***

Is this pie in the sky? Half the workers in this country use a computer on a network at the job. Is there some reason why those parents are denied the ability to communicate to their kids' teachers over those same networks? There's no good reason.

How is it working right now? We don't have the tools of connection, but we do have the following going on in this country: In terms of the information age, in terms of communications technology, we have home schooling for the rich.

That's what we have as a reality in this country. If you're well off, you've solved this problem already. You've bought a computer for your children, you've put them on a network, and things are going along pretty fast for those particular children. They're teaching themselves on those networks.

Two-thirds of the people in this country who earn more than $100,000 have networked personal computers for their children. We could say that's good enough. We could say, "We'll just settle for the market, that's the market at work." Or we could say, "Who are we kidding? This is not the country that we want our kids to grow up in." If we want anything close to equal opportunity for our children, we have to recognize that we don't want to close down our public schools, we want to change them. We want to make all of this available to all of our children. In addressing these problems, we need to find ways to break through some invisible barriers.

"It is absolutely essential that every classroom have some link to send and receive information."

What we have to do is equip all our classrooms with the tools to take advantage of the information revolution and then leave the classroom as a kind of nest, as a self-contained place, as a safe place. Schools will become a community center. I believe this will work very well.

Is there anyone who thinks that the wonderful technology of automobiles means that we should not invent car seats for children? Is there anyone who thinks that we should make sure that these schools are well run, but there shouldn't be any lunches in the schools for kids? Is there anyone who believes that the advances in society in some way should not be tailored to and adapted to the needs of our children? We don't believe this with respect to any advance in our society. We should not believe this with respect to the communications revolution. Bring it home to the kids.

Networked Classrooms Are an Achievable Goal

There is a now-familiar African proverb that says, "It takes a a whole village to raise a child." In this country, we have subsidies to insure that rural areas have phone service. I'm not against that. However, I do not understand why we should have this goal for Montana but not for our schools. I do not understand why we should be underwriting a second telephone line to the spa at the condominium in Aspen instead of to the teachers in the classrooms. And this is not hard to change. We can do both. We can make sure that affordable telephone service and communications service are made available to everyone in this country geographically, and also to everyone in this country by age, to teachers and to children. We don't need to limit it to the telephone companies. In the world of competition, many companies will be able to offer communications services. Computer companies, cable companies, many kinds of companies.

That's not the issue. The issue is our goals. For 60 years, as a country, we've had universal acceptance of the idea of universal service when it is a connection to the network. But we've left out schools and we can change this.

Now, I can't go back more than two decades and make up for the way I handled those 35 books in my first classroom. I can't make it up to those kids that I truly was not prepared for that job. I can't do that, and I can't make any of these things I'm talking about happen on my own. But I would like to ask educators to help me make it up to the children of those children and to all the other children in this world by taking these wonderful inventions and making them available to the next generation.

Computers Will Not Transform Education

by Michael Schrage

About the author: *Michael Schrage is a research associate at the Massachusetts Institute of Technology. He is the author of* No More Teams! Mastering the Dynamics of Creative Collaboration.

On practically every issue of import—Medicare, tax cuts, welfare reform—you'll find the President and the Speaker of the House bitterly and diametrically opposed. But when it comes to the future of education, the two enthusiastically agree: America's schools belong in cyberspace. Every classroom in the country should be wired to the Internet.

Excitement over the Internet and Education

"By being technologically smart . . . we can open up for these young people a very different future," asserted House Speaker Newt Gingrich (R-Ga.) at a newly wired elementary school in Washington, D.C., in May 1995. Speaking at San Francisco's Exploratorium science museum in September 1995, President Clinton heralded a public-private initiative to link the state's 12,000 elementary and high schools, comparing it to a "high-tech barn-raising." The Internet was cited as essential to bringing California's classrooms into the next century.

No, it's not. Sadly, the networks to educational hell are wired with good intentions. America's top two politicians are peddling a techno-vision that has virtually nothing to do with making schools better. The Internet is a fantastic, vibrant and evolving medium that will no doubt change the world. However, it is not a technology destined to improve our schools. This Internet infatuation offers a pathetic but telling symbol of just how badly the history and role of technology in education is misunderstood. This infatuation is about politics and pandering, not promise and potential.

Should Teddy Roosevelt have called for a telephone on every school desk and an operator in every classroom because Alexander Graham Bell's grand inven-

From Michael Schrage, "The Networks of Educational Hell Are Wired with Good Intentions," *Los Angeles Times*, October 8, 1995; ©1995, Los Angeles Times. Reprinted by permission.

tion was changing American society? Maybe "telephonic literacy" should have been enshrined in the 1910 school curricula? Would connecting America's classrooms have radically improved the quality of our great-grandparents' education and better prepared them for the rigors of the marketplace?

Perhaps John F. Kennedy—who obviously understood the transformative power of television—should have called on Americans to put a TV set in every classroom as well as a man on the moon. After all, television was destined to become the dominant communications medium of the generation. Why not rebuild American education around the television set? What's a public school classroom but a broadcast audience in miniature? Surely, American educators missed a golden opportunity to boost the quality of children's education by failing to creatively integrate TV into the schools.

> ***"[The Internet] is not a technology destined to improve our schools."***

Similarly, did President Ronald Reagan—The Great Communicator—cheat our schoolchildren by not aggressively pushing for scholastic cable hookups and VCRs? Why not a VCR and a television per child so that educational programs can be individually customized? After all, VCRs are standardized and far less expensive than computers. What's more, television, cable and VCRs are all "synergistic" technologies: they can run each other's software. They offer America a cost-effective technical infrastructure for our schools, no?

Past Technological Innovations Did Not Transform Education

Thinking people who care about children and know the sorry story of such technologies as television, calculators and language labs in the classroom would dismiss these historical hypotheticals as sheer nonsense. The idea that a telephone on every desk, a TV set in every classroom and a personal VCR for each child would have dramatically—or even incrementally—improved the level of elementary and high school education in this country is wishful thinking of the most destructive sort. It implies that the quality of education is predicated on the technological endowment of the school. That's like saying good school textbooks have a bigger impact on a child's education than good teachers. That may be true for a handful of students. However, school systems that celebrate the quality of their libraries and textbooks over the quality of their teachers, for example, are probably failing at providing a quality education for the bulk of their students.

What's so striking—and so sad—is that the Internet Infatuees swear that, this time, it's different. That—combined with the personal computer—the Internet will empower children to go to places they've never been, to link up with people all over the world, to tap into previously inaccessible resources etc., etc., etc.

Sorry—the Internet is just the latest technology that desperate educators, unhappy parents and pandering politicians have latched onto in hopes of avoiding the real problems confronting the schools.

Businesses and Schools Waste Money on Computers

It is a fact—not an opinion—that American companies have wasted tens of billions of dollars investing in information technologies that have yielded no improvements in productivity or innovation. Why? Because many of these companies didn't really understand either the impact of the technologies or how their organization would have to change to effectively use the technologies. The dirty, ugly little secret is that these companies have discovered that the root of their problems has little to do with technological competitiveness and everything to do with the way they managed themselves.

Similarly, the idea that Internet access is somehow an educational issue comparable to national standards, physical plant, classroom size, teacher quality, appropriate curricula and the ability to read represents an abdication of political leadership—not a visionary charisma. Indeed, the fact that our political leaders have made the Internet an educational issue shows how shallow our national conversation about education has become. Network technology is what you invest in after you have some idea of what you want an educational system to do and be—not before. Today's Internet Infatuation is emblematic of a society that would rather buy tools than go through the painful process of figuring out how to use them.

Sure, it's nice to have Internet access in the classroom—just like it's nice to have outlets in the classroom where you can plug in projectors and other educational appliances. But just as quality of education in the past wasn't dependent on electrical wall sockets, the quality of the educational future won't be dependent on digital Internet sockets. To argue that it should displays both an ignorance of history and a dishonesty about the real challenges facing the schools. The Internet isn't part of the solution; it's part of the problem.

Computers Cannot Replace Good Teachers

by Clifford Stoll

About the author: *Clifford Stoll is the author of* Silicon Snake Oil: Second Thoughts on the Information Highway.

Remember filmstrips? I used to look forward to Wednesday afternoons when our fifth-grade teacher would dim the lights, pull down the screen and advance the projector to an electronic beep. All the pupils loved filmstrips. For the next hour, we didn't have to think.

Filmstrips and Learning

Teachers liked them, too. With arms folded in the back of the class, they didn't have to teach. The principal approved. Filmstrips were proof that Public School 61 in Buffalo was at the cutting edge of educational technology. Parents demanded filmstrips, the modern, multimedia way to bring the latest information into the classroom. It was a win-win approach that bypassed textbooks and old-style classrooms. But no learning took place.

You've likely seen as many filmstrips as I have. O.K., name three that had a lasting effect on your life. Now name three teachers who did.

Yesterday's filmstrip has morphed into today's school computer. Promoted as a solution to the crisis in the classroom, computers have been welcomed uncritically across the educational spectrum. So uncritically that, astonishingly, school libraries, art studios and music rooms are being replaced by computer labs.

President Clinton promotes the wiring of the nation's high schools. Elementary schools seek grants for hardware and software. Colleges invest in video teaching systems. Yet the value of these expensive gizmos to the classroom is unproved and rests on dubious assumptions.

The Value of Teachers

What's most important in a classroom? A good teacher interacting with motivated students. Anything that separates them—filmstrips, instructional videos, multimedia displays, E-mail, TV sets, interactive computers—is of questionable education value.

Yes, kids love these high-tech devices and play happily with them for hours. But just because children do something willingly doesn't mean that it engages their minds. Indeed, most software for children turns lessons into games. The popular arithmetic program Math Blaster simulates an arcade shoot-'em-down, complete with enemy flying saucers. Such instant gratification keeps the kids clicking icons while discouraging any sense of studiousness or sustained mental effort.

Plop a kid down before such a program, and the message is, "You have to learn the math tables, so play with this computer." Teach the same lesson with flash cards, and a different message comes through: "You're important to me, and this subject is so useful that I'll spend an hour teaching you arithmetic."

Keys to Education

Computers promise short cuts to higher grades and painless learning. Today's edutainment software comes shrink-wrapped in the magic mantra: "makes learning fun."

Equating learning with fun says that if you don't enjoy yourself, you're not learning. I disagree. Most learning isn't fun. Learning takes work. Discipline. Responsibility—you have to do your homework. Commitment, from both teacher and student. There's no short cut to a quality education. And the payoff isn't an adrenaline rush but a deep satisfaction arriving weeks, months or years later.

Anyway, what good are these glitzy gadgets to a child who can't pay attention in class, won't read more than a paragraph and is unable to write analytically?

Still, isn't it great that the Internet brings the latest events into classrooms? Maybe. Perhaps some teachers lack information, but most have plenty, thank you. Rather, there is too little class time to cover what's available. A shortage of information simply isn't a problem.

There's a wide gulf between data and information. The former lacks organization, content, context, timeliness and accuracy. The Internet delivers plenty of data and precious little information. Lacking critical thinking, kids are on-screen innocents who confuse form with content, sense with sensibility, ponderous words with weighty thoughts.

> ***"Anything that separates [good teachers from motivated students] . . . is of questionable education value."***

Sure, students can search the Web, gathering information for assignments. The result? Instead of synthesizing a report from library sources, they often take the short cut, copying what's on line.

It's no surprise when a ninth grader turns in a history paper duplicated from a CD-ROM encyclopedia or a college sophomore turns in an English composition taken straight from the Internet. The copy-and-paste mentality of computing works against creativity.

Computing encourages the tyranny of the right answer. But the price of rigid thinking is whimsy lost, inventiveness snubbed, curiosity thwarted. Learning doesn't quantify well and it shouldn't be a competitive sport. Students who can explain their reasons for picking wrong answers contribute more to classroom dialogue than those who seldom make errors. To my way of thinking, mistakes are more interesting than correct answers. And problems more important than solutions.

"What exactly is being taught using computers? . . . That legible handwriting, grammar, analytic thought and human dealings don't matter."

Refuting Arguments for Classroom Computers

Promoters of the Internet tell us that the World Wide Web brings students closer together through instant communications. But the drab reality of spending hours at a keyboard is one of isolation. While reaching out to faraway strangers, we're distanced from classmates, teachers and family. Somehow, I feel it's more important to pen a thank-you note to a friend than to upload E-mail to someone across the ocean.

One of the most common—and illogical—arguments for computers in the classroom is that they'll soon be everywhere, so shouldn't they be in schools? One might as well say that since cars play such a crucial role in our society, shouldn't we make driver's ed central to the curriculum?

Anyway, computer skills aren't tough to learn. Millions have taught themselves at home. In school, it's better to learn how Shakespeare processed words than how Microsoft does.

The Gosh-Wow attitude of multimedia turns science and math into a spectator sport, substituting pictures of test tubes for the real thing. Which teaches more: watching a video about the heat of crystallization or dissolving potassium nitrate in water and touching the side of the beaker?

What exactly is being taught using computers? On the surface, pupils learn to read, type and use programs. I'll bet that they're really learning something else. How to stare at a monitor for hours on end. To accept what a machine says without arguing. That the world is a passive, preprogrammed place, where you need only click the mouse to get the right answer. That relationships—developed over E-mail—are transitory and shallow. That discipline isn't necessary when you can zap frustrations with a keystroke. That legible handwriting, grammar, analytic thought and human dealings don't matter.

Looking for simple ways to help in the classroom? Eliminate interruptions from school intercoms. Make classes smaller. Respect teachers as essential professionals with tough jobs. Protest multiple-choice exams which discourage writing and analytic thinking. If we must push technology into the classroom, let's give teachers their own photocopiers so they can avoid the long wait in the school office.

For decades, we've welcomed each new technology—stereopticons, lantern slides, motion pictures filmstrips and videotapes—as a way to improve teaching. Each has promised better students and easier learning. None has succeeded. Except that it is even more expensive, I suspect that classroom computing isn't much different.

Computers Cannot Teach Children Basic Skills

by David Gelernter

About the author: *David Gelernter is a professor of computer science at Yale University.*

Over the last decade an estimated $2 billion has been spent on more than 2 million computers for America's classrooms. That's not surprising. We constantly hear from Washington that the schools are in trouble and that computers are a godsend. Within the education establishment, in poor as well as rich schools, the machines are awaited with nearly religious awe. An inner-city principal bragged to a teacher friend of mine recently that his school "has a computer in every classroom . . . despite being in a bad neighborhood!"

Computers Teach Some Things Well

Computers should be in the schools. They have the potential to accomplish great things. With the right software, they could help make science tangible or teach neglected topics like art and music. They could help students form a concrete idea of society by displaying on-screen a version of the city in which they live—a picture that tracks real life moment by moment.

In practice, however, computers make our worst educational nightmares come true. While we bemoan the decline of literacy, computers discount words in favor of pictures and pictures in favor of video. While we fret about the decreasing cogency of public debate, computers dismiss linear argument and promote fast, shallow romps across the information landscape. While we worry about basic skills, we allow into the classroom software that will do a student's arithmetic or correct his spelling.

Computers Lower Reading Skills

Take multimedia. The idea of multimedia is to combine text, sound and pictures in a single package that you browse on screen. You don't just *read* Shakespeare; you watch actors performing, listen to songs, view Elizabethan buildings. What's wrong with that? By offering children candy-coated books, multimedia is guaranteed to sour them on unsweetened reading. It makes the printed page look even more boring than it used to look. Sure, books will be available in the classroom, too—but they'll have all the appeal of a dusty piano to a teen who has a Walkman handy.

So what if the little nippers don't read? If they're watching Olivier instead, what do they lose? The text, the written word along with all of its attendant pleasures. Besides, a book is more portable than a computer, has a higher-resolution display, can be written on and dog-eared and is comparatively dirt cheap.

"While we worry about basic skills, we allow into the classroom software that will do a student's arithmetic or correct his spelling."

Hypermedia, multimedia's comrade in the struggle for a brave new classroom, is just as troubling. It's a way of presenting documents on screen without imposing a linear start-to-finish order. Disembodied paragraphs are linked by theme; after reading one about the First World War, for example, you might be able to choose another about the technology of battleships, or the life of Woodrow Wilson, or hemlines in the '20s. This is another cute idea that is good in minor ways and terrible in major ones. Teaching children to understand the orderly unfolding of a plot or a logical argument is a crucial part of education. Authors don't merely agglomerate paragraphs; they work hard to make the narrative read a certain way, prove a particular point. To turn a book or a document into hypertext is to invite readers to ignore exactly what counts—the story.

The real problem, again, is the accentuation of already bad habits. Dynamiting documents into disjointed paragraphs is one more expression of the sorry fact that sustained argument is not our style. If you're a newspaper or magazine editor and your readership is dwindling, what's the solution? Shorter pieces. If you're a politician and you want to get elected, what do you need? Tasty sound bites. Logical presentation be damned.

Another software species, "allow me" programs, is not much better. These programs correct spelling and, by applying canned grammatical and stylistic rules, fix prose. In terms of promoting basic skills, though, they have all the virtues of a pocket calculator.

In Kentucky, as the *Wall Street Journal* reported, students in grades K–3 are mixed together regardless of age in a relaxed environment. It works great, the *Journal* says. Yes, scores on computation tests have dropped 10 percent at one school, but not to worry: "Drilling addition and subtraction in an age of calculators is a waste of time," the principal reassures us. Meanwhile, a Japanese educator informs University of Wisconsin mathematician Richard Akey that in his country, "calculators are not used in elementary or junior high school because the primary emphasis is on helping students develop their mental abilities." No wonder Japanese kids blow the pants off American kids in math. Do we really think "drilling addition and subtraction in an age of calculators is a waste of time"? If we do, then "drilling reading in an age of multimedia is a waste of time" can't be far behind.

Prose-correcting programs are also a little ghoulish, like asking a computer for tips on improving your personality. On the other hand, I ran this viewpoint through a spell-checker, so how can I ban the use of such programs in schools? Because to misspell is human; to have no idea of correct spelling is to be semiliterate.

Conditions on the Use of Computers

There's no denying that computers have the potential to perform inspiring feats in the classroom. If we are ever to see that potential realized, however, we ought to agree on three conditions. First, there should be a completely new crop of children's software. Most of today's offerings show no imagination. There are hundreds of similar reading and geography and arithmetic programs, but almost nothing on electricity or physics or architecture. Also, they abuse the technical capacities of new media to glitz up old forms instead of creating new ones. Why not build a time-travel program that gives kids a feel for how history is structured by zooming you backward? A spectrum program that lets users twirl a frequency knob to see what happens?

"We should not forget what computers are. . . . They are devices that help children mobilize their own resources and learn for themselves."

Second, computers should be used only during recess or relaxation periods. Treat them as fillips, not as surrogate teachers. When I was in school in the '60s, we all loved educational films. When we saw a movie in class, everybody won: teachers didn't have to teach, and pupils didn't have to learn. I suspect that classroom computers are popular today for the same reasons.

Most important, educators should learn what parents and most teachers already know: you cannot teach a child anything unless you look him in the face. We should not forget what computers are. Like books—better in some ways, worse in others—they are devices that help children mobilize their own resources and learn for themselves. The computer's potential to do good is modestly greater than a book's in some areas. Its potential to do harm is vastly greater, across the board.

Bibliography

Books

James Brook and Iain A. Boal, eds.	*Resisting the Virtual Life: The Culture and Politics of Information.* San Francisco: City Lights, 1995.
Daniel Burstein and David Kline	*Road Warriors: Dreams and Nightmares Along the Information Highway.* New York: Dutton, 1995.
Martin Campbell-Kelly and William Aspray	*Computer: A History of the Information Machine.* New York: BasicBooks, 1996.
Douglas Coupland	*Microserfs.* New York: ReganBooks, 1995.
Mark Dery	*Escape Velocity: Cyberculture at the End of the Century.* New York: Grove Press, 1996.
Mark Dery, ed.	*Flame Wars: The Discourse of Cyberculture.* Durham, NC: Duke University Press, 1993.
Andrew Feenberg and Alastair Hannay, eds.	*Technology and the Politics of Knowledge.* Bloomington: Indiana University Press, 1995.
Bill Gates	*The Road Ahead.* New York: Viking, 1995.
Joan M. Greenbaum	*Windows on the Workplace: Computers, Jobs, and the Organization of Office Work in the Late Twentieth Century.* New York: Cornerstone Books/Monthly Review Press, 1995.
Lawrence K. Grossman	*The Electronic Republic: Reshaping Democracy in the Information Age.* New York: Viking, 1995.
Katie Hafner and Matthew Lyon	*Where Wizards Stay Up Late: The Origins of the Internet.* New York: Simon & Schuster, 1996.
Katie Hafner and John Markoff	*Cyberpunk: Outlaws and Hackers on the Computer Frontier.* New York: Simon & Schuster, 1995.
Steven G. Jones, ed.	*CyberSociety: Computer-Mediated Communication and Community.* Thousand Oaks, CA: Sage Publications, 1995.
Thomas K. Landauer	*The Trouble with Computers: Usefulness, Usability, and Productivity.* Cambridge, MA: MIT Press, 1995.

Richard A. Lanham — *The Electronic Word: Democracy, Technology, and the Arts.* Chicago: University of Chicago Press, 1993.

Tracy L. LaQuey with Jeanne C. Ryer — *The Internet Companion: A Beginner's Guide to Global Networking.* Reading, MA: Addison-Wesley, 1993.

William J. Mitchell — *City of Bits: Space, Place, and the Infobahn.* Cambridge, MA: MIT Press, 1995.

Frank Ogden — *Navigating in Cyberspace: A Guide to the Next Millennium.* Toronto: MacFarlane, Walter & Ross, 1995.

Howard Rheingold — *The Virtual Community.* Reading, MA: Addison-Wesley, 1993.

Herbert I. Schiller — *Information Inequality: The Deepening Social Crisis in America.* New York: Routledge, 1996.

Steven L. Talbott — *The Future Does Not Compute: Transcending the Machines in Our Midst.* Sebastopol, CA: O'Reilly and Associates, 1995.

John Tiffin and Lalita Rajasingham — *In Search of the Virtual Class: Education in an Information Society.* New York: Routledge, 1995.

Sherry Turkle — *Life on the Screen: Identity in the Age of the Internet.* New York: Simon & Schuster, 1995.

Periodicals

Ian Angell — "Winners and Losers in the Information Age," *Society*, November/December 1996.

Herb Brody — "Internet@Crossroads.$$$," *Technology Review*, May/June 1995.

Gary Chapman — "Flamers," *New Republic*, April 10, 1995.

Mark Chen — "Pandora's Mailbox," *Z Magazine*, December 1994.

Kenneth W. Dam and Herbert S. Lin — "National Cryptography Policy for the Information Age," *Issues in Science and Technology*, Summer 1996.

Esther Dyson et al. — "A Magna Carta for the Knowledge Age," *New Perspectives Quarterly*, Fall 1994.

Barbara Ehrenreich — "Put Your Pants On, Demonboy," *Time*, October 23, 1995.

Philip Elmer-Dewitt — "On a Screen Near You: Cyberporn," *Time*, July 3, 1995.

David Futrelle — "Safety Net," *In These Times*, August 7, 1995.

James Gleick — "Crasswords," *New York Times Magazine*, April 16, 1995.

Laurie Hays — "PCs May Be Teaching Kids the Wrong Lessons," *Wall Street Journal*, April 24, 1995.

Andrew Kupfer — "Alone Together: Will Being Wired Set Us Free?" *Fortune*, March 20, 1995.

Carl S. Ledbetter Jr. "Take a Test Drive on the Information Superhighway," *Vital Speeches of the Day*, July 1, 1995.

Steven Levy "The Case for Hackers," *Newsweek*, February 6, 1995.

Steven Levy "The Luddites Are Back," *Newsweek*, June 12, 1995.

Abigail McCarthy "Cyber Campus?" *Commonweal*, April 7, 1995.

Chris Morton "The Modern Land of Laputa Where Computers Are Used in Education," *Phi Delta Kappan*, February 1996.

Hamid Mowlana "The Internet Elite," *Bulletin of the Atomic Scientists*, July/August 1995.

Nicholas Negroponte "Pluralistic, Not Imperialistic," *Wired*, March 1996. Available from 520 Third St., 4th Fl., San Francisco, CA 94107.

Erik Ness "BigBrother@Cyberspace," *Progressive*, December 1994.

Christopher Scheer "The Pursuit of Techno-Happiness," *Nation*, May 8, 1995.

Daniel J. Silver "Computers and Their Discontents," *Commentary*, July 1995.

Julian Stallabrass "Empowering Technology: The Exploration of Cyberspace," *New Left Review*, May/June 1995.

Douglas Stanglin with Josh Chetwynd "Technology Wasteland," *U.S. News & World Report*, January 15, 1996.

Louis Uchitelle "What Has the Computer Done for Us Lately?" *New York Times*, December 8, 1996.

Gerard van der Leun "Twilight Zone of the Id," *Time*, Spring 1995.

Organizations to Contact

The editors have compiled the following list of organizations concerned with the issues debated in this book. The descriptions are derived from materials provided by the organizations. All have publications or information available for interested readers. The list was compiled on the date of publication of the present volume; names, addresses, phone numbers, and e-mail/Internet addresses may change. Be aware that many organizations may take several weeks or longer to respond to inquiries, so allow as much time as possible.

Center for Civic Networking (CCN)
PO Box 65272
Washington, DC 20037
(202) 362-3831
fax: (202) 986-2539
e-mail: ccn@civicnet.org

CCN is dedicated to promoting the use of information technology and infrastructure for the public good, particularly for improving access to information and the delivery of government services, broadening citizen participation in government, and stimulating economic and community development. It conducts policy research and analysis and consults with government and nonprofit organizations. The center publishes the weekly *CivicNet Gazette.*

Center for Democracy and Technology (CDT)
1001 G St. NW, Suite 700 E
Washington, DC 20001
(202) 637-9800
fax: (202) 637-0968
e-mail: info@cdt.org
Internet: http://www.cdt.org

CDT's mission is to develop public policy solutions that advance constitutional civil liberties and democratic values in new computer and communications media. Pursuing its mission through policy research, public education, and coalition building, the center works to increase citizens' privacy and the public's control over the use of personal information held by government and other institutions. Its publications include issue briefs, policy papers, and *CDT Policy Posts,* an on-line, occasional publication that covers issues regarding the civil liberties of those using the information highway.

Center for Media Education (CME)
1511 K St. NW, Suite 518
Washington, DC 20005
(202) 628-2620
fax: (202) 628-2554
e-mail: cme@access.digex.net

CME is a public interest group concerned with media and telecommunications issues, such as educational television for children, universal access to the information highway, and the development and ownership of information services. Its projects include the Campaign for Kids TV, which seeks to improve children's education; the Future of Media, concerning the information highway; and the Telecommunications Policy Roundtable of monthly meetings of nonprofit organizations. CME publishes the monthly newsletter *InfoActive: Telecommunications Monthly for Nonprofits.*

Computing Research Association (CRA)
1875 Connecticut Ave. NW, Suite 718
Washington, DC 20009
(202) 234-2111
fax: (202) 667-1066

CRA seeks to strengthen research and education in the computing fields, expand opportunities for women and minorities, and educate the public and policymakers on the importance of computing research. CRA's publications include the bimonthly newsletter *Computing Research News.*

Electronic Frontier Foundation (EFF)
PO Box 170190
San Francisco, CA 94117
(415) 668-7171
fax: (415) 668-7007
e-mail: eff@eff.org
Internet: http//www.eff.org

EFF is an organization of students and other individuals that aims to promote a better understanding of telecommunications issues. It fosters awareness of civil liberties issues arising from advancements in computer-based communications media and supports litigation to preserve, protect, and extend First Amendment rights in computing and telecommunications technologies. EFF's publications include *Building the Open Road, Crime and Puzzlement,* the quarterly newsletter *EFFector Online,* and on-line bulletins and publications, including *First Amendment in Cyberspace.*

Electronic Privacy Information Center (EPIC)
666 Pennsylvania Ave. SE, Suite 301
Washington, DC 20003
(202) 544-9240
fax: (202) 547-5482
e-mail: info@epic.org
Internet: http//www.epic.org

EPIC advocates a public right to electronic privacy. It sponsors educational and research programs, compiles statistics, and conducts litigation. Its publications include the biweekly electronic newsletter *EPIC Alert* and various on-line reports.

Institute for Global Communication (IGC)
18 De Boom St.
San Francisco, CA 94107
(415) 442-0220
fax: (415) 546-1794
e-mail: support@igc.apc.org

The institute provides computer networking services for international communications dedicated to environmental preservation, peace, and human rights. IGC networks include EcoNet, ConflictNet, LaborNet, and PeaceNet. It publishes the monthly newsletter *NetNews.*

Interactive Services Association (ISA)
8403 Colesville Rd., Suite 865
Silver Springs, MD 20910
(301) 495-4955
e-mail: isa@aol.com

ISA is a trade association representing more than three hundred companies in advertising, broadcasting, and other areas involving the delivery of telecommunications-based services. It has six councils, including Interactive Marketing and Interactive Television, covering the interactive media industry. Among the association's publications are the brochure *Child Safety on the Information Superhighway,* the handbook *Gateway 2000,* the monthly newsletter *ISA Update,* the biweekly *Public Policy Update,* and the *ISA Weekly Update* (delivered by fax or e-mail).

International Society for Technology in Education (ISTE)
University of Oregon
1787 Agate St.
Eugene, OR 97403
(800) 336-5191
fax: (503) 346-5890

ISTE is a multinational organization composed of teachers, administrators, and computer and curriculum coordinators. It facilitates the exchange of information and resources between international policymakers and professional organizations related to the fields of education and technology. The society also encourages research on and evaluation of the use of technology in education. It publishes the journal *Computing Teacher* eight times a year, the newsletter *Update* seven times a year, and the quarterly *Journal of Research on Computing in Education.*

National Library of Education
555 New Jersey Ave. NW, Rm. 101
Washington, DC 20208-5721
(800) 424-1616
fax: (800) 219-1696
e-mail: Library@inet.ed.gov
Internet:http://www.ed.gov

The library provides specialized subject searches and retrieval of electronic databases. Its other services include document delivery by mail and fax, research counseling, bibliographic instruction, interlibrary loan services, and selective information dissemination. For those who have access to the Internet, the library provides general information about the Department of Education, full-text publications for teachers, parents, and researchers, and information about initiatives such as GOALS 2000, Technology, and School-to-Work Programs.

National School Boards Association (NSBA)
1680 Duke St.
Alexandria, VA 22314
(703) 838-6722
fax: (703) 683-7590
Internet: http://www.nsba.org/itte/

The association is a federation of state school boards. NSBA advocates equal opportunity for primary and secondary public school children through legal counsel, research studies, programs and services for members, and annual conferences. It also provides information on topics such as curriculum development and legislation that affects education. NSBA endorses the use of computers as an educational tool. The association publishes the bimonthly newsletter *A Word On,* the monthly *American School Board Journal,* the biweekly newspaper *School Board News,* and numerous other publications.

Office of the Vice President of the United States
Communications Office
Old Executive Office Bldg., Rm. 272
Washington, DC 20501
(202) 456-7035
fax: (202) 456-2685
Internet: http://www.whitehouse.gov

Under the leadership of U.S. vice president Al Gore and others, together with the Office of Science and Technology Policy and other federal offices, the White House in 1994 unveiled a program called "Welcome to the White House: An Interactive Citizens' Handbook," which is accessible on the World Wide Web, a feature on the Internet. Accessible material includes detailed information about cabinet-level and independent agencies and commissions, a subject-searchable index of federal information, and "hotlinks" to related areas of interest.

Special Interest Group for Computers and Society (SIGCAS)
c/o Association for Computing Machinery
1515 Broadway, 17th Fl.
New York, NY 10036
(212) 869-7440
fax: (212) 944-1318

SIGCAS is composed of computer and physical scientists, professionals, and other individuals interested in issues concerning the effects of computers on society. It aims to inform the public of issues concerning computers and society through such publications as the quarterly newsletter *Computers and Society.*

Index